D0483568

Praise for *The Pet Poo Pocket Guide*

Whether you're looking to safely manage your own pet's waste or revolutionize the way we handle our nations', this book is for you. With humor, passion and years of experience, Seeman offers greener disposal solutions that will frankly leave you excited to scoop! A one-of-a-kind guide that every pet owner or solid waste manager must own.

—Aimee Christy, Research Scientist,
Pacific Shellfish Institute, Olympia, WA

In this concise, engaging, and often humorous guide, Seeman provides an array of options for sustainable pet waste disposal and upcycling. With contagious enthusiasm and no-nonsense pragmatism, the author encourages us to overcome the "ick factor" and be proactive in reducing our pets' "carbon paw prints". There's enough technical detail and scientific background to satisfy the composting geek, explained in down-to-earth language accessible to the general reader.

—Sami Gray, landscaper/nurserywoman/botanist,
Washington State

The
Pet Poo
pocket guide

How to safely compost and
recycle pet waste

Rose Seemann

new society
PUBLISHERS

Copyright © 2015 by Rose Seemann.
All rights reserved.

Cover design by Diane McIntosh.
Cover images © iStock
Main image © iStock ma_rish Flies & hearts © iStock Nenochka

Printed in Canada. First printing April 2015.

Inquiries regarding requests to reprint all or part of *The Pet Poo Pocket Guide* should be addressed to New Society Publishers at the address below. To order directly from the publishers, please call toll-free (North America) 1-800-567-6772, or order online at www.newsociety.com

Any other inquiries can be directed by mail to: New Society Publishers
P.O. Box 189, Gabriola Island, BC V0R 1X0, Canada
(250) 247-9737

LIBRARY AND ARCHIVES CANADA CATALOGUING IN PUBLICATION

Seemann, Rose, author
The pet poo pocket guide : how to safely
compost and recycle pet waste / Rose Seemann.

Includes index.
Issued in print and electronic formats.
ISBN 978-0-86571-793-0 (pbk.). ISBN 978-1-55092-588-3 (ebook)

1. Compost. 2. Animal waste—Recycling. 3. Pet cleanup.
I. Title.

TD796.5.S44 2015   631.8'75   C2014-907941-9
                          C2014-907942-7

This book is intended to be educational and informative. It is not intended to serve as a guide. The author and publisher disclaim all responsibility for any liability, loss or risk that may be associated with the application of any of the contents of this book.

The interior pages of our bound books are printed on Forest Stewardship Council®-registered acid-free paper that is 100% post-consumer recycled (100% old growth forest-free), processed chlorine-free, and printed with vegetable-based, low-VOC inks, with covers produced using FSC®-registered stock. New Society also works to reduce its carbon footprint, and purchases carbon offsets based on an annual audit to ensure a carbon neutral footprint. For further information, or to browse our full list of books and purchase securely, visit our website at: **www.newsociety.com**

To Gretchen and Max

"Nature does have manure and she does have roots as well as blossoms, and you can't hate the manure and blame the roots for not being blossoms." — Buckminster Fuller

Contents

Good intentions but clueless

"Do your business, Gretchen!" 2

Dealing with dog doo:
a speed-of-light history 5

Cat poo: another story altogether 10

How did I get into this crap? 12

Piled higher and deeper 15

You take it. No, YOU take it. 24

Oh, ick...NOT! 27

Before we start:
Five more preliminary items

Hazards 36

Start with healthy dogs and cats 41

Location, location, location 42

The great pickup bag charade 45

Heavy metals and pharmas 49

And so we begin:
Best practices for pet waste recycling

"Recycle" vs. "upcycle" 54

Flushing 57

Burial 62

Biodigestion/septic bin 68

Bokashi (Essential Microorganisms/EM) ..73

Composting..84
Moldering...105
Vermiculture (cultivating worm poop)....109

Mission possible:
"gold star" DW compost

Down the rabbit hole 124
Plant power unleashed 135
Conclusion...148
Notes 154
Acknowledgements 157
Index 158
About the author 165

Chapter One

Good intentions
but clueless

"Do your business, Gretchen!"

This November morning was way too wet and cold to be stomping around the "back forty" for any appreciable time. I looked at my watch: 7:23. If I didn't get on the road by 7:30, I'd be late for work on a Monday — always a bad move.

Gretchen was not a stupid dog. She was a shepherd who didn't like to be hurried. The place, the smells, the mood had to be just right before she deposited her treasure with Mother Earth. I had to remain calm or I'd botch the entire enterprise.

"Do your business, Gretchen!" I repeated firmly, giving her leash a few gentle tugs.

She sniffed a rotting tree stump and shoved her snout into a clump of grass with a bit of green lingering at the center. 7:24. This was not going to be an easy morning.

I'm more than a little embarrassed to say it, but when Gretchen refused to focus on the business at hand, I would sing to her. Yes, sing. Right out there in the sleet, right there in my hooded trench coat and clunky rubber boots.

She was partial to slow, melodic tunes with lots of cadence. This morning I decided to pull a guaranteed hit out of my walkies playlist: "Save Your Heart for Me" by Gary Lewis and the Playboys. I sang this song when I soothed her, brushed her fur and ran her bathwater. If you sing a song and nobody except your dog is there to hear it, is it really so crazy?

Was it the little whistle at the start of that song that she loved? I whistled the intro softly and then crooned:

"Walk along the lake with someone new / Have yourself a summer fling or two / But remember I'm in love with you / And save your heart for me."

She looked up at me with peaked brows. I could see Gretchen's resolve melting.

"When the summer moon is on the rise / And you're dancing under starlit skies / Please don't let the stars get in your eyes / Just save your heart for me."

Of course she expected all four choruses, which fit nicely into my four-minute window.

"Please remember I'm in love with you / So save your heart for me / Darling, sa-a-a-ve your heart for me."

So Gretchen did her business. I said, "Good girl!" and her licorice lips curved into a smile.

She knew all along what I wanted her to do. But the song was an understood token of exchange. I gave so she gave. Silly, softie me. Gretchen is gone, but after all these years, I still cry on cue if that song crosses my mind.

So did I pick up after our Gretchen? The "back forty" where she did her business wasn't really forty acres. That's just what we called the 20-by-40-foot strip of wooded

property at the end of our back lawn. By the time the deed was done, I had exactly two minutes to slog back to the house, settle Gretchen inside, lose the boots, whip on the high heels and head off to work.

So what did I do with the doo? I made sure that my husband Chuck and our young son Greg walked very carefully around the "back forty" until we had a chance to clean it up. That didn't happen until spring, six months after we welcomed Gretchen to our house in a suburb north of Pittsburgh. This first reconnaissance and assault resulted in a large plastic tub filled with dog waste. Mission accomplished. But how should we dispose of the payload?

Now I have an abiding respect for garbage collectors and the work they do. I did not want to throw this crap into plastic bags and leave it at the curb. What if it exploded in the compactor, spewing poop shrapnel in all directions? It was too grim to consider.

Since the exercise was taking on the bearing of a military campaign, Chuck suggested that we dig a latrine. So we simply carved out a long, shallow trench and buried Gretchen's waste. We did this year after year — spring and fall — as part of the seasonal yard work. Would I do it that way again? Well, no.

The property sloped down to a creek within view of the

Rose Seemann

trench, so poopy runoff was a distinct possibility. Maybe
the pathogens and nitrogen in the waste simply dissipated
in the soil and did no harm. Or maybe the pollutants
seeped into the groundwater and into the stream and
into the Allegheny River. But if damage was done, it was
done long ago by a family who meant well but Just Didn't
Know Better.

Dealing with dog doo:
a speed-of-light history

And why would they have known better? Back in the
day, public health messages about pet waste were
pretty basic: "Don't touch it. Wash your hands right away
if you do. Don't let baby play with it or eat it. Dog doo is a
stinky toxin. You could go blind or die. Oh, ick. Stay as far
away as possible."

But that wasn't easy to do.

There was a time when city dogs ran free. They did
their business anywhere they had a mind to and it wasn't
your job to pick it up. Your job was to not step in it. One
early public service message was "Curb Your Dog," which
meant urging your pet to "go" in the street near the curb.
Then — bingo! — the next rainstorm could sweep that
stockpile of poo down the nearest gutter. Once in a city's
storm sewer, it made its way into nearby waterways, i.e.,

your beach, your recreational river or lake, your drinking water. That worked out nicely.

Decades after "Don't Be a Litter Bug," people-who-should-know told us to "Scoop the Poop." This idea took a while to catch on, but catch on it did — much to the delight of plastic poop bag manufacturers and Pet People eager to feel good about recycling shopping bags. And it caught on just in time to help manage the droppings of an onslaught of pampered pooches.

According to the American Pet Products Association (APPA), the number of dogs in the United States increased from 75 million two years earlier to 77.5 million in 2009–10. There is now one dog for every four people. Without stoop-and-scoop and dog parks, we city folk would be spending a good part of the day scraping crap off our shoes, possibly our ankles. As it is, around 60 percent of Dog People now pick up their dog's poop. Another good percentage left at ground zero is removed thanks to the kindness of strangers.

But wait — is this the end of the story? Most pet stewards have been well trained to pick up after their dogs ("Good girl; good boy!"). From the looks of things, a lion's share of the nasty stuff has disappeared from our byways. But you don't need to have a PhD in physics to know that it doesn't simply vanish. Remember that exploding poop shrapnel? Dog waste, tons and tons of it, is still being packed into garbage trucks and hauled off to its final resting place in the landfill. R.I.Poo.

Don't even get me started on landfills! Have you ever toured a landfill? They are not happy little dumps with seagull haloes where the trash is consumed by the dirt to create heavenly soil under future subdivisions. There has never on God's green Earth been a dump like that. But this is most people's idea of a landfill.

Years ago dumps were simply smelly open pits where trash was buried — cafeterias for rats, mice and other scavengers. Over time, water leached through the contents, polluting nearby groundwater and sometimes poisoning pristine aquifers. But that's no longer the case. Today's sanitary landfills are specially designed structures in which engineered liners seal trash off from surrounding water, air, soil and rain.

Under these conditions, trash remains intact indefinitely. For "regular" decomposition by an ordinary-good-guy mix of microorganisms to occur, some oxygen needs to be present. Landfills are designed to be solid, compact and oxygen free. So organics simply sit there for a long time — forever, as far as anyone can tell, except that they are decomposed a little by special microorganisms that can live without

oxygen. This slow-motion demo crew gives off methane instead of carbon dioxide, the by-product produced by the regular-good-guy microorganisms.

Organics, including pet waste, degrade in landfills via anaerobic critters that live without oxygen and produce methane. This powerful greenhouse gas then seeps out and is ultimately released into the air through pipes and valves built into the landfill. Municipal solid waste (MSW) landfills are the third largest source of human-related methane emissions in the United States, accounting for approximately 17.5 percent of all these emissions in 2011.[1]

We have the technology to tap some of this gas as a power source. The US Department of Energy encourages recovering landfill gas and offers grants from the American Recovery and Reinvestment Act (ARRA) of 2009. But tapping it depends on whether authorities and businesses have the will and financing to invest in the necessary equipment.

A thousand years from now archaeologists might be working these sites like King Tut's tomb, finding our cabbage heads, Pokemon chips and plastic-shrouded dog turds still intact. They will wonder which of these objects were tools, which were fetishes and which were strictly ornamental.

Concluding that the mummified poop was used as a

currency would be a good guess. There is so much of it! Plus the DNA of crap and greenbacks is similar, and the packets easily fit into your pocket. But the sizes vary. Did the larger ones have greater value? And these treasures are all so carefully wrapped and knotted in petroleum-based encasements. The Ancients must have believed that the mummified brown knobs had great value.

I have gone off the deep end with this little story. But not so deep that we can't dig our way out and get back to the point. The point being: once trainable Dog People cleaning up after their pets start thinking about where it goes and what happens to it, they have eaten Forbidden Fruit from the Tree of EcoKnowledge. Once we Know Better, we are cast forever out of the Garden of EcoIgnorance. And there is no turning back from Niggling Understanding. We can only choose to disregard it, deny it, make excuses or fix things for the better.

Deciding to "fix things for the better" leads to the next logical step: cycling your pet's waste back to the Earth. Landfills sealed with liners are a half-measure for any organic material. According to the EPA, these liners will eventually crack.[2] Think system failure. Think earthquake. Think tectonic shifts.

The Wisconsin Department of Natural Resources states: "Current landfill designs and practices do not

provide for degradation of landfilled organic wastes within a defined and reasonable timeframe. Un-degraded organic wastes can potentially cause future environmental or economic impacts if the landfill gas and leachate collection and containment systems (cap and/or liner) fail at some time in the future. Potential economic burdens and environmental risks associated with these un-degraded wastes will be largely borne by future generations."

Sad but true.

Cat poo: another story altogether

"Bring in the dog and put out the cat. Yakety yak (don't talk back)." Back in '58 when this Coasters song hit the airways, even city people routinely put out the cat at night. Kitty might return in the morning with a shredded ear, peculiar carcasses and fleas, but it was considered rather cruel not to let felines out to have their nefarious nighttime fun. And more years passed before Cat People felt the need to indulge kitties with their own indoor loos. The commercial production of clay litters and specially molded plastic boxes helped to seal the deal on indoor litter boxes.

Furthermore, today's Cat People have a better appreciation of the dangers waiting to pounce on their pets just beyond the doorstep. Or maybe the world just seems like a bigger, badder place. Busy highways are but a stone's throw from residential neighborhoods. As suburbs encroach on hunting grounds, wild predators desperate for food pose real threats. As do Mean People everywhere. There are fewer hiding places. And we want to give our cats a chance to live all the nine lives their DNA has dealt them. Outside of rural mousers, most "owned" cats today are indoor or mostly-indoor pets.

Even in the days when city cats spent much of their time outdoors, we weren't tripping over cat waste. Cats are fastidious creatures. A cat doesn't poop in public on a whim like a Canada goose. Felines like their privacy and cover up after themselves on most occasions. But as anyone who cleans a litter box knows, their calling cards still pile up.

According to a study done by the US Department of Agriculture, the typical dog generates ¾ of a pound (340 g) of waste a day — or 275 pounds (125 kg) per

year. This author and her Cat People friends found that an average cat produces significantly less poop every day: a carbon paw print of a third of a pound (150 g), if you factor in clumping clay litter. Yes — we weighed it. That makes a single cat's annual output 110 pounds (55 kg).

Let's put this whole cat waste vs. dog waste thing in perspective right now: dog waste is a much bigger nuisance than cat waste. Dog waste is public, it is destructive, it piles up in gargantuan proportions. So we will be spending much of our time dealing with the many social and environmental complications related to dog doo. But this book will give the cats equal time when it comes to recycling solutions.

How did I get into this crap?

The Denver area is teeming with dogs. Walk in any park and you'll see them, every breed and combination of breeds known to man, parading like four-legged princes with stewards in tow. Two, three, four dogs tethered with clever lead arrangements are not uncommon. Talk to many of these Multi-Dog People and they will tell you that they believe dogs are happier in packs or that they want to adopt as many dogs as they can manage — just to give them homes forever. These reasons are truly edifying.

Across a park pathway you're likely to see a willowy

runner bending over to pick up after her vizsla. A little farther along a walker is doing a disappearing act with his cockapoo poo. Scan a panorama and you'll see Dog People bobbing up and down like the Heckle and Jeckle oil pumps you see dotting the prairie. Or like those drinking birds that delight children by dipping again and again over a glass of water. It just gets you to thinking.

In modern industrialized countries, human waste is flushed and treated, filtered and heated until it is safe enough to release or till back into the land. Whatever inefficiencies and absurdities are involved in the system, it's working for now, as long as the water supply holds out. Meanwhile here we are, wrapping our dog's turds in a piece of plastic and throwing them in the trash. How dumb is that?

There is no Barbara Woodhouse command that will stop healthy dogs from pooping. So how much of this stuff is out there? Are there better ways to handle this? Is anyone doing it? Is anybody even considering doing it?

These questions about how pet waste impacts the environment started nibbling away at the corners of my curiosity. I did a few casual online searches. Each answer made me more uncomfortable and led to more questions. Then I did some simple math and found out how a little scoop here and a little bagful there add up to Serious Tonnage.

That hooked me. Now the Dona Quixote of Doo, I made phone calls, exchanged e-mails and chalked up some miles to satisfy my curiosity. And I became convinced about the feasibility of turning dog waste into a safe and productive soil amendment.

I found a pet scoop pro and a composting wizard who were asking the same questions. We all wanted to know if we could turn this environmental liability into a garden gold legacy. Our dogwaste composting experiment produced a fragrant soil amendment that met EPA regulations and teemed with nutrients and the good biology that plants love (see below, Mission possible: "gold star" DW compost). Green Pet Compost in Oregon[3] and the Tompkins County Dog Owners Group in New York[4] successfully conducted similar projects. So this is a physically possible, physically replicable process. No one considered our unconventional composting sensational. What we were doing was not compelling or sexy, like a new cash-back credit card offer. But word slowly made its way to the local news media, blogs and online forums for dog, sustainability and gardening enthusiasts.

Eco-conscious pet stewards, scoopers, dog day care owners, pet sitters, veterinarians and park administrators all over the United States and Canada began visiting our EnviroWagg website and contacting us. Every one of them hoped that we had solutions to their hound and kitty mounds. So the dialogue began.

They asked us questions and we did our best to come up with solutions that would work for their situations. They told us in no uncertain terms what worked and what went over like poop shrapnel. And we're passing along this mother lode of data to you.

How to begin? Let's put on our hip boots and wade into some stats on sheer quantity.

Piled higher and deeper

If you pick up after your dog and deposit a little wrapped parcel into the nearest trash can, it seems like such a tiny contribution. A BM (bowel movement) this morning, another BM later in the day. You pick up. You are a good steward. Some jerks don't pick up at all. Sometimes you even pick up for them. These little presents don't seem like much in the grand scheme of garbagedom.

However, if you pitch waste from even one dog into your home trash, you know that it can be the heaviest item in the bag. On the plus side, your doo adds ballast that anchors your trash on a windy day. On the minus, you have a very real reminder of your pooch's carbon paw print. And it ain't pretty. The average dog produces 275 pounds (125 kg) of waste per year.

If you serve multiple dogs or pet sit, your reality checks multiply. If you run a scooper service, kennel, dog park, mush dog yard or vet clinic, pet waste can be 75 percent or more of your refuse. These are the folks who really do get to thinking and looking for practical solutions to an obviously mounting problem. Here's where theory becomes disposal dilemma.

Now I don't have a PhD in statistics, but I can handle simple math. Here's the real scoop on how much our dogs generate.

Dog stats

- 83 million dogs in US households (US Humane Society)
- On average, each dog produces 0.75 lb. of waste per day (US Dept. of Agriculture).
- 83 million dogs produce 62,250,000 lb. of waste per day.
- Divided by 2,000 = 31,125 tons per day.
- Times 365 = 11,360,625 tons (10,300,000 tonnes) per year.
- Let's be conservative, round it off and say 11 million tons (10 million tonnes) of dog waste per year.

What does that look like?

- 11M tons of dog waste = 22,000,000,000 lb. (22 G lb.)

- Dog waste weighs approximately 35 lb. per cu. foot (yes, we weighed it).
- 22,000,000,000 lb. of dog waste divided by 35 = 628,571,429 cu. ft.
- 628,571,429 cu. ft. covers 62,857,143 sq. ft. and is 1 ft. deep.

How many football fields does that cover each year?

- 1 football field (including end zones) = 57,600 sq. ft.
- 62,857,143 sq. ft. divided by 57,600 sq. ft. = 1,091 football fields 1 ft. deep or 109 football fields 10 ft. (3 m) deep.

Of course, we're not tipping the entire contents of these football fields into landfills. Let's overlook dog waste in rural areas where the need for pickup is not vital to sanitation and sanity. Country dogs have always been happy-go-lucky rascals when it comes to pooping. They have so much space for romping, they deposit their calling cards like wild animal scat — more social networking than nuisance.

Chances are good you won't run into country canine doodles unless you're doing some serious tracking. And Mother Nature happily gathers that well-dispersed poo into the folds of her big loving skirts. On the other hand, in urban areas with populations greater than 30,000, around 60 percent of the community's dog waste is scooped and trashed. What does that look like?

Let's take Colorado as an example. As the 22nd most populous state in the United States, it's right around the middle of the pack.

- 635,550 dogs in Colorado's 19 cities with populations of 30,000+
- On average, each dog produces 0.75 lb. of waste per day.
- 635,500 dogs produce 476,625 lb. per day.
- Divided by 2,000 = 238.3 tons per day.
- Times 365 = 86,984 tons per year.
- Times 60% = 52,190 tons (47,174 tonnes) picked up/streamed into landfills.
- The Statue of Liberty weighs 225 tons. 52,190 tons divided by 225 tons = 232.
- All the Colorado dog waste streamed into landfills each year weighs as much as 232 Statues of Liberty.

Now consider this: 50,000-plus tons of the state's dog excrement per year adds up to a very, very, very gargantuan pig lot or stockyard or dairy farm. If you could locate a poo bomb this massive in a single location on Google Earth, it would scream for regulation and treatment. But you can't, so it doesn't.

How does dog waste stack up against other waste streams? A recent audit found that pet waste makes up 3.8 percent of the garbage from residential collections in San Francisco.[5] In 2006, the City of Toronto found that dog waste is the largest litter stream by weight in its public parks.[6] The popularity of off-leash dog parks is growing big time. Our collection experience has shown that trash bins at these sites often contain 85 percent dog waste.

In 2006 Colorado disposed of 34,000 tons of #1 and #2 plastics. That's 34,000 tons of used plastics vs. 50,000+ tons of dog waste. Recycling programs diverted 20 percent of #1 and #2 plastics from landfills.[7] So what's the plan for the 52,194.27 tons of dog waste generated annually? Sadly, there isn't one.

Plastic recycling is more energy intense than organics recycling practices such as composting. Many forward-leaning cities and towns are recycling yard waste and food scraps. Unlike metals, glass and plastics, these organics release large amounts of the methane released from landfills during the slow anaerobic decomposition process. But the same cities are ignoring pet waste. Is this simply because it's … icky? Communities focusing on reaching zero-waste goals will need to find solutions for this non-traditional waste stream that do not include denial.

Cats outnumber dogs but generate less waste. When you add clumping clay litter, each cat contributes around one third of a pound (150 g) of waste to daily trash. Since there is no way to calculate the amount of cat waste deposited in indoor litter boxes vs. outdoors, let's look at simple kitty poo production. Like dogs, the cats are hard at work.

Cat stats

- 96 million cats in US households
  (US Humane Society)
- On average, each cat produces 0.3 lb. of waste/litter residue per day.
- 96 million cats generate 28,800,000 lb. of waste per day.
- Divided by 2,000 = 14,400 tons per day.
- Times 365 = 5 million tons (4.5 million tonnes) per year
- That's 500,000 dump trucks full of cat poop.
- There are no statistics on how much cat waste is streamed into landfills.
- A recent American Bird Conservancy (ABC) telephone survey indicates that 65 percent of all respondents believe that keeping cats indoors is safer and healthier for cats.

Now check this data on Colorado's city cats — pets most likely to use litter boxes and have their waste trashed.

- 717,000 cats in Colorado's 19
  cities with populations of 30,000+
- On average, each cat produces 0.3 lb. of waste/litter residue per day.
- 717,000 cats produce 205,100 lb. per day.
- Divided by 2,000 = 102.55 tons per day.
- Times 365 = 37,430.75 tons per year streamed into landfills

- Let's add that total to the 52,194.27 tons of trashed dog waste from Colorado's 19 cities with populations of 30,000+
- 37,430.75 tons of cat waste + 52,194.27 tons dog waste = 89,625.02 tons of pet waste.

What does that look like?

- The Washington Monument weighs 81,120 tons.
- The Statue of Liberty weighs 225 tons.
  89,625.02 tons = one Washington Monument + 37 Statues of Liberty.
- All the Colorado urban dog and cat waste streamed into landfills each year weighs as much as one Washington Monument + 37 Statues of Liberty.

The Internet offers online credit calculators that tally household carbon footprints. Determining factors include home square-footage, energy use, number of residents and travel. Why no mention of pets?

Kitty footnotes

Can cat waste be recycled the same ways as dog waste? For the most part, yes. The big difference is that dog waste is collected in plastic pickup bags and cat waste mixes with litter. Both of these commingled materials complicate recycling practices, and we will explain these complications. But you can recycle both waste streams the

same way and take similar precautions when dealing with the potential for canine- and feline-specific pathogens.

Just to keep things simple, every solution for dog waste recycling in this book also applies to cat waste — with three important feline exceptions.

1. Quit the clay

Do not use clay-based cat litter if you plan to recycle cat poop. Clay will not decompose, and may inhibit the process and contaminate the resulting material. Look for corn-, wheat-, wood- and paper-based litters that will break down with other organic materials. An economical option is small animal-bedding pine pellets. Many people suggest slowly adding the pellets to familiar clay litters to entice cats to switch. But our cat Max quit clay cold turkey and accepted pellets almost too enthusiastically. He seems to like the smell of fresh pine. And this litter eliminates odor.

The staff at the feed store where we buy our animal bedding told us that quite a few locals use it as cat litter. Cleaning a litter box with pellets takes a bit of finesse, but is easy if you use an extra-wide (5 inch/12 cm) and deep litter scooper. Simply scoop out the poop and toss it into a waste bag. Then scoop up some of the urine-dampened pellet chunks and sift the sawdust into the same bag.

Throw the dry pellets back into the box. The litter box smells great, the pellets last a long time and the poop and sawdust compost beautifully! See "Adapting dog/cat waste composting to space and climate."

Environmentalists and holistic pet stewards criticize clay litter for being unfriendly to the earth because sodium bentonite, a popular constituent of clump cat litter, is obtained through strip mining. They also say that the substance is unhealthy for pets. Commercial litter often contains crystalline silica and various chemical concoctions to reduce odor. Other respected sources refute these negative claims against clay litter. The war of words will continue as long as there is money to be made manufacturing and marketing litter. These issues aside, for recycling purposes, do not use clay.

2. Do not flush cat waste

Keep cat waste away from all water sources as the feces may contain Toxoplasma gondii, a disease agent toxic to sea otters. A California law[8] requires commercial litter to include warnings such as, "Please do not flush cat litter in toilets or dispose of it outdoors in gutters or storm drains." If you live east of the Rockies, your water flows to water uninhabited by otters. But we

don't know if T. gondii affects other species of marine mammals, so why not be cautious?

So much for flushable cat litter and training kitty to perch on the toilet seat.

3. Do not deposit cat waste in doggie septic/biodigestion systems

Dog-waste septic systems use anaerobic microorganisms to break down material in environments with little air, such as tanks. Septic starters are often added to promote natural bacterial growth. When the process flows along smoothly, the waste liquefies and is absorbed into the ground. Even plant-based litters can slow down the progress and clay litter will bung up the works entirely. So resist the urge.

You take it. No, YOU take it.

Waste management companies have been playing hot potato with pet waste and disposable diapers for decades. Agencies can't agree on what to do with it. These organics are in the Twilight Zone of disposal management. This Canadian city's story is not uncommon.

"Some jurisdictions ban animal waste in domestic garbage as a potential health hazard since neither storage nor means of transfer nor destination is planned or designed for this type of material. This is also true of Vancouver landfills, which specifically state that 'all forms of excrement are prohibited from garbage disposal.'"[9]

Commercial and municipal composters that routinely handle yard waste and even food scraps normally refuse to take pet waste for "health and sanitation reasons." These professionals are always on their toes maintaining a proper balance of carbon, nitrogen, air, heat and moisture, so that the aerobic process moves merrily along. Who wants to throw in a monkey-wrench material that might result in more extensive monitoring, more odors, more scavengers, exotic pathogens and disgruntled neighbors?

Of course, regardless of warnings and rules, pet poop slithers its way into the waste stream. Where else can it go? Dog People and Cat People will continue to disregard the warnings and wrap it up with the trash. They will continue to rake it into bags for recycling yard waste and toss it into bins for composting food scraps. Once pitched, this contraband crap will be properly processed like bathtub gin at a speakeasy. But isn't it time to end the silly contradictions?

Public health agencies and municipalities are all over the map when it comes to advice on pet waste disposal.

Some recommend that the stuff be double-bagged, pitched in the trash and never, ever composted. Others sponsor classes on how to recycle pet poo. Momentum appears to be on the side of official approval — and even encouragement — of safe practices that divert pet poop from landfills.

The Environmental Protection Agency (EPA) says that agencies can suggest flushing dog waste down the toilet.[10] Better check out potential snafus in the "Flushing" section.

Eco-conscious community leaders who see the zero-waste handwriting on the wall are taking the initiative in pet waste recycling. Officials in a number of cities are piloting programs that process all food scraps, yard waste and other compostable materials normally considered too contaminated to be recycled: meat, cheese, bones, greasy paper plates ... and pet waste. Others are dog park pioneers.

Sustainability-minded Dog People in Ithaca, New York, maintained a dog waste composting program for several years that greatly reduced the tons of trashed raw feces their pets produced and turned it into compost that was safe and nutritious for plants. Volunteers at Notre-Dame-de-Grâce Dog Run in Montreal operate an ongoing dog waste-composting program that was the subject of a Concordia University study.[11] Pacific Dog Park in Cambridge, Massachusetts, hosted the Park Spark Project,[12] an interactive art installation featuring a biodigester tank that converted dog waste into electricity to light the park.

Massive biodigesters have the advantage of producing useful residual material plus refuse-derived fuel (RDF). The City of Toronto has one of a growing number of public and privately operated large-scale digesters. These systems might provide the ultimate solution for dealing with nontraditional organic waste. See the sidebars "City of Toronto's green bin program" and "The Park Spark Program," both in the "Biodigester/septic bin" section.

Oh, ick … NOT!

Let's get this over with early on. Drop the poop phobia right now. Get a grip on the gag reflex. No OCD tailspins, please. If you want to recycle organics, you need to think like a techno-geek, not a loosey-goosey sixth grader.

Smelly stuff really, really, really repulses us — with good reason. Smelly stuff is associated with any organic material that is in the process of being digested by a microbial playground of protozoa, bacteria and fungi. If this degradation and transformation did not occur, life as we know it would simply not be possible.

These microscopic critters don't whistle while they work like the Seven Dwarfs. The ones that live in places

with no air (think waterlogged, sopping wet places) emit gases that we would describe as "putrid." Microbes are so numerous, ubiquitous and diverse that just thinking about this amazing mini-universe can give you brain freeze. But some of them can poison us if we ingest them, so we have been hardwired to react with immediate aversion. Oh, ick! This is not the end of the microscopic critter story.

Mostly we see microbes in masses as mold on cheese or scum in the birdbath. But their many cousins are so versatile that they survive in every part of the biosphere, from the deepest ocean trenches to the highest mountains. Microbes live literally everywhere on Earth and even in the atmosphere. They are essential to our planet's life cycle, eternal scavengers that decompose everything that once lived and plow it back into new life.

People with a scientific bent spend entire lifetimes studying microbes. They teach courses, conduct research, publish tracts and speak at conferences. The Web gives them a platform to exchange information at online forums. If you want to know more about these cool microscopic creatures, go online and access academic resources plus lively discussions among highly accredited professionals.

Unscientific anecdotal litter byte
A volunteer at a shelter just west of Denver told me that

But for our purposes, just a few facts about microbes will help us weigh up our pet waste recycling options.

Each type of microscopic creature flourishes in its own comfort zone of heat, air and moisture — or lack thereof (love that word). Their little mojos grind to a halt when conditions around them change. At that point, a new species of tiny reinforcements rise up to take over.

A **mesophile** is an organism that grows best in moderate temperatures between 68 and 113°F (20 and 45°C). These organisms are the keys to mesophilic processes — making cheese, yogurt, pickles and sauerkraut, and fermenting alcohol. Think about it the next time you enjoy a kraut dog with beer or Brie with Chardonnay. But let's fast forward from gastronomy to pet waste disposal. This will take some effort on both our parts, but here goes.

In addition to mesophiles there are **thermophiles** — microbes that like it hot and flourish in temperatures between 113 and 252°F (45 and 122°C) provided they have the right amounts of oxygen and water. Generally speaking, mostly anaerobic mesophiles (remember, anaerobic means able to live in the total absence of oxygen) take care of business in flushing, burial, septic

feline respiratory problems decreased considerably when the facility switched from commercial clay litter to donated wood shavings.

and bokashi scenarios while thermophiles step in when conditions are right for high-heat composting.

Another important distinction is between "good" and "bad" microbes. Some deep thinkers have observed that there are no good people or bad people, just good actions and bad ones. Gardeners often say that weeds are only weeds in the eyes of the beholder. The same can be said about microorganisms. For instance, moldy foods contaminated with tremorgenic mycotoxins will help fuel the action in a compost pile. But if your dog eats even a small amount, these microbes will make it sick within a few hours. Depending on the dose, Fido might even die.[13] So practically speaking, experts do need to make the call on whether a microorganism is generally good or bad for us and those we nurture.

Health care professionals know that microbial balance is essential to health. They can pinpoint bacteria and viruses that are dangerous to the well being of people, pets, wild animals and plants. Microorganisms that commonly wear black hats are called "**pathogens**." Think of them as the Lee Van Cleefs of the microscopic universe. Although nothing organic is entirely free of pathogens, our goal is to limit them and facilitate healthy processes.

At this point I also need to mention a fact you might already appreciate. All creatures with advanced digestive systems — including you and your pet — host a huge population of diverse microorganisms in their guts. These are essential for breaking down the foods that nourish us. This waste management brigade evolved eons before we did, literally enabling us to exist as we do and enjoy the life we live. But there's one little drawback in our relationship with microbes.

The reason that smelly stuff really, really, really repulses us is that people are (wisely) inclined to back off when they get a whiff of methane, which they say "stinks." This greenhouse gas is a necessary byproduct of anaerobic mesophilic microbial digestion. The bad smell tells us that potentially unfriendly microorganisms have called "dibs" on the food and are already working to degrade it.

That odor can be a lifesaver because some of the microbes might be pathogens that can make us very sick. (Wouldn't it be nice if our dogs were hardwired like that?) The smell intensifies in feces, which are crammed with millions of microorganisms busy digesting the food residue.

So our reaction to bad smells (or even the anticipation of bad smells) runs from "oh, ick" through a more profound "oh, yuck" to quiet repulsion, depending on our sensibilities. Can we move on to Oh, Ick … NOT? Please? Are we going to be led around by our noses or our brains? We change diapers. We pick up after pets. We clean the aquarium and the toilet. Why the drama?

the **Pet Poo** *pocket guide*

We apply mysterious man-made chemicals so that everything smells "springtime fresh," yet we seal what smells — but is truly the elixir of future life — in plastic and throw it into a hermetically sealed but somewhat leaky tomb that oozes methane for a long, long time. If we want to recycle pet waste or any other organic, we need to get over hyperhygiene at inappropriate times. Common sense cleanliness is a very commendable habit; a necessity, even. But hyperhygiene is for food prep, decontaminating astronauts and removing spleens.

No consistent public solutions

The EPA's most recent update to "Composting at Home" includes dog and cat waste in its list of "What NOT to compost," citing that it "might contain parasites, bacteria, germs, pathogens, and viruses harmful to humans." But it leaves policy and enforcement to local jurisdictions.

In National Pollutant Discharge Elimination System (NPDES), Pet Waste Management — the EPA states, "Deciding whether to encourage residents to dispose of pet waste in the trash, bury it in their yards, or flush it down the toilet is an important issue for communities." Local authorities might insist that residents double-bag and trash pet waste or they might provide incentives for recycling it. Here are some responses:

Composting Pet Waste: Cost Share Available, Rivanna Regional Stormwater Education Partnership, North Carolina ("Depending on where you live, there are two sources of cost share funding for pet waste composters.

Rose Seemann

As you approach the practices outlined here, think of tolerating, controlling and eliminating odors as the small price you pay to work as a partner with nature. It's the effort you contribute for taking responsibility for your pet's carbon paw print. Once you appreciate the multitudes of microorganisms and the yeoman's job they do for us, an "awe factor" should override the "ick factor."

Both programs will pay 50% of the cost of composter.")

Let's discuss Fluffy's pet waste, Snohomish County, Washington State ("Pet feces and cat litter can be put in the garbage ... double bagged in plastic and tied tightly.")

Pet Waste Composting Comes to Kingston, CKWS TV News, Kingston, Ontario, July 2013 ("If you have a dog — there is a way to safely dispose of your pet waste without harming the environment. A local group is holding seminars next month on composting the waste.")

Composting Questions and Answers, City of Houston, Official Site for Houston, Texas 2013 ("Do not compost pet waste. Not only are they smelly, but they can be dangerous to your health.")

Recycling center to put on composting event, *The Joplin Globe*, Joplin, Missouri, November 13, 2013 ("Members of the Chert Glades Master Naturalists will demonstrate how to make a dog waste digester.")

Chapter Two

Before we start:

Five more preliminary items

Hazards

Pets like rabbits, gerbils and hamsters are herbivores, so disposing of their poo is easy. Recycle it as you would food scraps or yard waste. Or bury it in the garden. Raw waste from dogs, cats and other meat-eating animals is too harsh for tender plants and more likely to carry pathogens.

But this stuff is not nuclear waste. Do you refuse a kiss from your pooch because you wonder where his loving snout has been? No. Do we have ongoing human epidemics due to our close contacts with pets? No. Do you know anyone who became violently ill because they share quarters with pets? Probably not. Widespread problems associated with dog and cat waste are more likely to be caused by pollution than health issues.

So, short of an impending natural disaster or a disaster in full swing or the aftermath of said disaster, there is never, ever an excuse for not picking up after your dog. Trashing poop is always better than leaving it where it lands.

Recent studies show that dogs are third or fourth on the list of "nonpoint source" (i.e., diffuse; point sources are things like factories and sewage treatment plants) contributors to bacteria in contaminated waters, increasing the potential for serious diseases, including cholera and dysentery. According to the EPA, two days' worth of raw dog waste runoff from about a hundred dogs can create enough pollution to close a bay and all the watersheds within 20 miles (36 km).

Waste left on the ground — no matter how far away from a storm drain or stream — can eventually end up polluting a waterway. In addition to threatening health, bacteria that feed on dog waste deplete oxygen in water, killing native aquatic life. The bacteria also produce algae blooms that block sunlight and suffocate fish.

In arid locations with little drainage, dog waste left intact can take more than a year to break down. Left along trails it can morph into fertile patches that invite invasive weeds, crowding out fragile native plants. If you are a serious hiker who takes your dog roaming far from trash cans, invest in one of the many odor-proof packs or containers designed to help you "pack it out."

Health experts point to the potential microbes in infected raw dog waste such as coccidia, giardia, hookworms, parvovirus, Toxocara canis roundworms (ascarids) and whipworms. An average dog dropping also contains three billion fecal coliform bacteria. When dogs infected with roundworms leave their droppings on the ground, viable eggs can linger in the soil for years.

Cats are the primary hosts of feline-specific parasites, including T. gondii, which can cause toxoplasmosis, a

serious and occasionally fatal illness to infants, pregnant women and people with compromised immune systems. Like roundworms, these oocysts are extremely difficult to kill, but like roundworms, they can be destroyed at a sustained temperature of 122°F (50°C) — a heat achieved via successful composting.[14]

Outdoor cats that dine on mice are most likely to be carriers,[15] but don't give your indoor cat a free pass. Our indoor cat Max does a kitty crab walk when an outside door opens, but I once found a mangled mouse behind my computer tower.

So there is a chance that your pet might carry pathogens. Always give raw dog and cat waste its props. Give the poo its due. But understand that the dangerous microorganisms it might contain will only give you health issues if you ingest it or rub it into your eyes or open skin.

Handle pet waste in a respectful way, whether or not your goal is cycling it back to nature. Wash your hands if there is any possibility of contact. Keep equipment used to recycle pet waste separate from equipment used to recycle material for edible gardens. This will eliminate cross-contamination. Do not process dog or cat waste in open areas where it can be accessed by children, pets or wildlife.

Never use raw pet waste to topdress soil where fruits (including berries) or vegetables may drop and later be harvested from the ground. Plant roots do not uptake pathogens and transport them to other portions of the plant. But the pathogens can easily survive on the surface of edibles.

Although some proponents maintain that bokashi and vermiculture practices eliminate pet waste pathogens, there is no guarantee that do-it-yourself (DIY) practitioners will be able to fully destroy enough harmful parasites to make the product safe for edible gardens. One sure way to kill these pathogens without outside chemical intervention is to fully compost them.

Dr. T. Gibson, head of the Department of Agricultural Biology at the Edinburgh and East of Scotland College of Agriculture, is the authority often quoted as the final word on destroying pathogens through composting. He stated, "All the evidence shows that a few hours at 120 degrees Fahrenheit (49°C) would eliminate them completely. There should be a wide margin of safety if that temperature were maintained for 24 hours."

Large-scale sewage treatment and recovery, which sometimes later includes composting, can process sewer biosolids (read: human waste and industrial/chemical runoffs) so that the material meets EPA standards for commercial sales and agricultural usage. The resulting material must be tested and meet agency requirements for pathogen densities.[16]

Flushing or burial gets you off the hook in terms of reusing the end product. So does biodigestion using a septic tank if you do not harvest residue. But if you casually recycle pet waste using bokashi, composting, moldering or vermiculture, there is no guarantee that your end product will be safe. Sooo …

Do not use DIY pet-waste recycling compost, vermicompost (worm poop), digested sludge or leachates/teas on or near edible crops. No matter how carefully you handle the process, unfinished material might be mingled with the finished product. If you drop your fruits or vegetables onto your recycled fertilizer while harvesting or if bits of soil cling to tubers, you might be exposed to harmful pathogens.

That said, your finished DIY soil amendment can be green dynamite for outdoor or indoor ornamental plants. You will have nutrition-packed soil at no cost and divert your household pet waste from the local landfill: Smaller Carbon Paw Prints.

Are you afraid that health department agents are lurking, waiting to send in a SWAT team if you recycle your pet's waste? Frankly, they have much bigger fish to fry. Unless you pollute a stream, defile a public recreation spot, create unhealthy conditions resulting in sickness, disturb your neighbors or leave a mess for someone else to clean up, you are a free agent. Only if your activities qualify you as a bona fide nuisance will your local health department act and be commended for a job well done.

Start with healthy dogs and cats

Feed your pets with care. Garbage in, garbage out. The type of food you give your pets will affect not just their health, but also the quality and quantity of waste you must deal with. The easier food is to digest, the more completely it will be digested, resulting in smaller stools that will decompose faster.

Foods based on meat and rice are easiest to digest. Soy- and wheat-based foods aren't bad, but corn-based food doesn't break down well. If a food isn't easy to digest, the resulting waste will not break down easily either. Read pet food labels carefully and consult with your vet about the nutritional value of specific diets.

Regular visits to the vet ensure that parasites are not hitching a ride with your pets, compromising their health and contaminating feces. Follow a worming schedule developed by a veterinarian familiar with local conditions. Puppies and kittens that have not been dewormed are almost always carriers.

There is no way that most of us can absolutely monitor what our pets eat. Dogs will chomp down irresistible but iffy stuff as they explore. Cats kept indoors will occasionally snag an unlucky intruder. But chances are good that a healthy pet's waste will not contain dangerous bacteria and parasites that can easily transmit disease.

Location, location, location

Does your dog do his business on your property or offsite? If you are going to recycle waste using any of these practices, it will be much easier for you to scoop up the poo immediately and start the process. Your dog will generally defecate within a quarter mile (400 meters) of the start of a walk, so it might save time in the long run to

Herbivores vs. carnivores

The Denver Zoo has a long history of sustainable practices. For years the zoo transported its tons of animal waste to a regional composting yard. But the composters only accepted herbivore poop because of the complications involved in safely processing the waste of meat-eaters. The carnivore and omnivore waste was routinely trashed.

The zoo now operates a biomass gasification system that uses high heat to convert all of its solid waste into renewable energy. The poo even powers a maintenance vehicle! This program saves the zoo thousands of dollars annually and provides a model project for public facilities.[17]

get him or her in the habit of using your yard or another appropriate nearby site for toilet purposes and then moving on for walkies.

That doesn't give your canine buddy free rein to turn your bluegrass into Swiss cheese. If you have some out-of-the way space in your yard, you can set aside a "pooch patch" and train your dog to only transact serious business at that spot.

Dogs are attracted to pooping places with longer grass. A restricted "wild" area with grass four or more inches (ten or more centimeters) tall works best and has the added advantage of reduced mowing. The most dog-tolerant grasses tend to be perennial ryegrasses and fescues. Pick up the poo right away and douse the grass with water if possible.

Dog waste vs. plutonium

Dog day care owners, poop scoopers, pet sitters and shelters are the multi-dog stewards who contact us most with questions about keeping waste out of dumpsters. Many say that they do not have the time, space or resources to recycle the waste. I always ask if there is a large waste treatment plant or biodigester nearby that might accept the waste. A woman in charge of a rescue group in North Carolina replied, "Nothing like that ... but we do have a nuclear power plant down the road." We shared some laughs about the favorable cost-benefit analysis of nuclear energy that produces toxic waste versus the dimmer prospects of a biodigester fueled by toxic waste.

Your pet will usually want to urinate before deciding to dump the whole enchilada. Repeatedly urinating on a single spot will kill any type of grass or other ground cover, so you might want to add a slightly modified area at or near your pooch patch for this purpose.

Some European dog parks use a pee pole setup to confine urination, but for some reason the practice has not been adopted in the United States. Simply install a pole in the center of a designated area and surround it with a scattering of sand or pea gravel (get it?). Female dogs may be just as comfy squatting on a nice sandy place without the pole.

Introduce your dog to the patch right away and continue to accompany him to the spot for "visits." Sing his praises or give him a treat for performing like a champ. Your pet will get the idea and return to use the patch for its intended purpose on his own. You might need to reinforce this behavior if your dog has a contrary nature or simply wants to piss you off (pun intended).

If cajoling and commands fail to work, try banging a pot or simply clapping just as your pet begins settling down to business on forbidden turf. The peace and quiet of the pooch patch will look much more attractive. The American Society for the Prevention of Cruelty to Animals (ASPCA) provides excellent training instructions, under the title "Teaching Your Dog to Eliminate in a

Specific Place," in the Pet Care section of its website.

Be sure to place your patch close to a trench, bin, tank or other outdoor recycling system so that cleanup will be easy. If you pick up waste offsite, hauling it back for recycling will add another step to the process. You might decide it's too much trouble or just too darn far to transport your pet's waste and simply trash it in the nearest bin. Or you might think it's worth the effort. In either case, you will need a bag.

The great pickup bag charade

You've seen the claims about dog bags that:

- compost like autumn leaves
- degrade in landfills
- leave no trace

I talked to a woman so sure of this packaging hype that she left her full doo bags right out in the middle of a dog park field. "When I come back, the bags are always gone because they're biodegradable," she said. She was convinced that they had morphed into dirt overnight.

Some well-meaning Dog People believe that, contrary to the laws of nature, biodegradable bags will disintegrate in a landfill and the contents will push up daisies right through tons of trash. Many manufacturers are shameless when it comes to justifying overcharging for

For starters, when you throw your dog poo into the trash, who cares how it's wrapped? It's going to be sealed in a landfill where it will go into suspended animation. When you purchase a commercial dog-bag product — whether it is ordinary plastic, "biodegradable" or even "certified compostable"— you are responsible for creating another bag. Isn't it better for the environment to simply reuse a bag that's already been created?

Poly bags touted as "biodegradable" contain additives that cause the plastic to become brittle and then break into pieces. These pieces get smaller and smaller until they cannot be seen. Did they biodegrade or is this a case of out-of-sight-out-of mind? Aren't the bits just becoming

Plastic or paper?

FEDOG of Prague, Czech Republic, has a solution that is both smart and gracious. The company manufactures an "environmentally-friendly bag for dog excrement." Their bags are made of recycled paper. Each bag contains a strip of cardboard that Dog People easily fold into a scooper. Both scooper and waste can be slipped back into the bag and folded up for on-the-spot disposal.

plastic dust, waiting for an opportunity to enter the food chain at a microbial level?

Compostable bags are primarily made of biodegradable polyesters and renewable resources such as starch. It's complicated, but suffice to say that that bag made from corn is not all corn or it would not "hold together" as a film. And even if it is primarily corn or potatoes or beets, aren't those things we should be eating … or distilling? You're probably thinking that there's no way around the plastics dilemma. But wait, what's this? (See "Plastic or Paper" below.)

Now back to better living through polymers. There is no good–better–best when it comes to dog bags made with plastic film. But here are some tips:

* If you trash pet waste, simply use shopping or newspaper bags.

FEDOG launched the product in 1994 and was granted a patent for the EU in 2004. Physically handicapped workers in protected workshops help in the final production. Each year this company distributes many thousands of these bags, steel dispensers and stands to parks all over Europe and Asia.

(Never stop believing that people with insight, good intensions and determination can be agents for positive change.)

- If you trash pet waste and need additional bags, buy pickup bags made of recycled plastic.
- If you send poo back to nature using burial or composting, you can use a certified compostable bag (American Society for Testing and Materials — ASTM 6400), tearing open the film if possible. Or use a paper bag. Or tear pickup sheets out of the Yellow Pages … as in, improvise! Breaking open the bags before burial or composting is helpful. Some compostable bags take a long time to degrade.
- If you send poo back to nature using biodigestion (pet septic system), bokashi, moldering, vermiculture or bokashi, use no bags. Flushable bags are an option for flushing.

California law trashes "biodegradable" bag claims

On October 8, 2012, California Governor Jerry Brown signed a bill that prohibits the sale of plastic bags labeled "'biodegradable,' 'degradable,' or 'decomposable,' or any form of those terms." Furthermore, "... while scientific technical standards exist to verify that a product is 'compostable,' there are no such standards to verify if a product is 'biodegradable' because the conditions and timeframe inherent in the claim of 'biodegradability' are too vague."[18]

Rose Seemann

Heavy metals and pharmas

"The heavy metals when linked to organic matter have a behavior in the soil that is still little known."[19] Manure commonly contains cadmium, copper, zinc or other compounds at various levels depending on the amount of heavy metals in the diet and the environment. Yet commercial farmers commonly use treated sewage biosolids (read: human feces) to fertilize their crops. They also apply manure from cows, pigs and chickens.

The EPA has set limits for specific metals before processed sludge can be used for agricultural processes. But a wide variety of heavy metals remains at certain levels, so the heavy metal cycle continues, biosolids to foods to fertilizers to biosolids.

Yin and yang of plastic

I have used the word "plastic" 54 times in this book — not just to criticize its environmental impact, but also to suggest solutions. Plastic is cheap and everywhere. Pet waste recycling should be easy, so I will be suggesting readers use plastic storage bins for wormeries, plastic compost tumblers, plastic bokashi buckets, plastic garbage cans for pet-waste septic tanks, plastic moldering containers and more. Nothing works quite as well as plastic to keep water in or out. But use it judiciously. Create less new plastic — reuse, reuse and reuse again before recycling.

Ditto residual pharmaceuticals and hormones from meds that are routinely prescribed for animals and humans alike. We know that these contaminants move through the food chain, often unaltered. Regulations limit some of them, but this stuff is building up faster than kudzu in monsoon season. There are enough data and opinions on this subject to fill many volumes. We could spend our lives trying to keep track.

Should you be paranoid about this? Only if you're paying attention. I'm not an expert on the subject, but when

Humble solution for heavy metals

Researchers from the Pondicherry University in India discovered that earthworms can significantly decrease levels of heavy metals such as cadmium, copper, lead, manganese and zinc from municipal solid waste. Microorganisms in the worms' digestive systems pull heavy metal ions from material passing through. The metals then become locked in the worms' tissue. When the worms are removed, the vermicompost is safe for agricultural use. [20]

Time and *Consumer Reports* start exploring it with lead articles, I get antsy.

So please, don't talk to me about heavy metals or meds as they relate to pet poop recycling. Don't go off the deep end about immortal miniscule vinyl polymer strands in dog bags that might make their way into doggie compost. Insidious soil contamination is an issue that needs to be addressed in high-level scientific and policy circles, not *The Pet Poo Pocket Guide*.

Humble mission

Our goals here are cutting down on volume, pollution and landfill fodder, and repurposing perfectly useful organic material. Taking care of our own pet's business is a first step and something each of us can do. You might say it's (oh, no and duh!) "doo-able."

Chapter Three

And so we begin:

Best practices for
pet waste recycling

The Earth neither grows old or wears out if it is dunged. — Columella, circa 45 A.D.

Now we're getting down to business. No more "poop," "poo" or "doo" or clever references to defecation or elimination. And I am so tired of the words "waste" and the highly denigrating "crap." Any material with the potential to spin off nitrogen, phosphorus and potassium, the building blocks of plant life, and the ability to fuel zoo maintenance vehicles is a "windfall."

So I will use the initials DW, CW and D/CW for the stuff I previously termed "dog waste," "cat waste" and "dog/cat waste."

~~Dog waste~~ Dog windfall = **DW**

~~Cat waste~~ Cat windfall = **CW**

~~Dog and/or cat waste~~ Dog and/or cat windfall = **D/CW**

Instead of using the word "recycle" when referring to D/CW, I will switch to the more apt term "upcycle."

Recycle Upcycle

"Recycling" is a process that changes or reconditions an item that is no longer useful into a product of further use. Much of inorganic recycling is "downcycling," that is, turning the material into a substance with less value than it originally possessed. Plastics and metals are examples of materials commonly downcycled.

That's not the case with organics, which can be easily upcycled. Upcycling is a process that transforms the item into something more valuable than it was at the start. "An upcycled material not only pays back, but pays back with dividends!"[21]

Of the many advertised D/CW upcycling products and systems, some are truly useful and others are gimmicks and wastes of money. Some work well under one circumstance but are poop bloopers under others. None of these systems are "silver bullets" that will solve D/CW issues with absolutely no effort on your part. Someone is trying to sell them, for Pete's sake, so they will look very slick and easy.

For these reasons, we will be taking a DIY approach, sometimes alluding to manufactured items but not discussing the merits of specific products. If a practice mentioned here looks like it might work for you, simply go online and search "dog waste" + "composting" or "dog waste" + "vermiculture" etc. as keywords. You'll find detailed instructions, personal experiences and, yes, many ingenious commercial products that might help. From there, let common sense be your guide.

One more time!

Do not use raw D/CW, unfinished or finished residue from your processing on or near fruits or vegetables. None of the DIY practices described in this book are guaranteed to result in compost for use on plants grown for humans to eat. Use degraded residues only on or around ornamentals — decorative plants such as trees, shrubs, grasses or flowers.

Fruits and vegetables, particularly tubers, may come into contact with the residue directly and retain pathogenic microorganisms, even if cleaned. Only carefully monitored commercial processing followed by EPA-approved testing will assure you that a D/CW fertilizer is safe for food production.

New warning!

Do not stockpile D/CW. Begin processing as soon as possible. Dealing with too much material at one time will lead to trouble in any of these practices. A responsible steward understands that nature works slowly. Its magic can't be rushed or overburdened, but can be managed if understood.

Each of the practices below starts with quick summaries, listed in order of difficulty. To avoid leaky basements,

E. coli contamination and incredulous plumbers, please read through the entire section before trying any of the options.

Sometimes using several practices, managed simultaneously or sequentially, will work best for you. For instance, if you experience seasonal freezes, you might flush in the winter and bury when the soil is workable. Or you might add digestion or bokashi sludge to a D/CW compost pile. Consider the pros and cons and home in on a practice that looks promising for your situation. Then give it a go. If it doesn't work, try another. If it does work out, tweak it so it works even better!

Flushing

Start up: easy

Learning curve: easy

Maintenance: easy

Need: flush toilet or other outlet connected to sanitary sewer (NOT septic tank)

Helpful: scooper, "flushable" bags

Advantage: best for indoor dogs; physically challenged or small dogs

Disadvantage: transporting DW from outdoors can be messy; potential for clogged plumbing. Do not flush cat waste!!

Take away: good eco vibes

According to the EPA, flushing DW down the toilet is a viable disposal option.[10] Toilet waste flows into sanitary sewers (not storm sewers) and winds up at plants that treat the material to control dangerous pathogens. Sanitized water can be reused and sludge is sometimes repurposed as agricultural fertilizer. But there are mixed opinions and technical complications involved in flushing.

On the one hand, many newer animal shelters routinely hose loose raw DW from holding areas into septic sewerage drains. These drains are designed right into facility plans for that purpose. On the other hand, some municipalities have ordinances that ban pet waste flushing. Treatment facilities themselves are iffy. Call your local plant and ask about flushing your own pet's DW. They will give you thumbs up or thumbs down depending on their outlook and capacities.

And who can blame the plant staff when they "just say no?" If flushing pet waste ever caught on, the trend would put an additional burden on treatment systems. The plants were designed to handle quantifiable amounts of human waste. Exactly what would an x factor of DW mean for operations?

And what if streams of DW-filled plastic bags shushed into their aeration lagoons? Would each plant be forced to deal with a mini Pacific Garbage Floating Patch? These municipal waste pros always have their eyes on the end game.

Let's say you decide to go ahead and flush DW with or without official blessing. Seems to you like a great idea that will work. But there are limitations. You can't just drop a neatly knotted bag full of DW into the toilet, flush and count on the best outcome.

Using a regular plastic bag is never acceptable. Do you really want to foist a bag that will never degrade in a meaningful time frame onto your treatment plant? To further complicate things, your toilet may reject your kind offering. Yes, that bag may not even make it to its destination because the plastic is likely to bung up your plumbing. Oh, ick.

Those who are not faint of heart can collect DW in plastic or paper bags and tip it into the toilet. This is a less than ideal operation that involves extra handling. And now you have to dispose of the soiled bags. And clean the DW-tainted toilet bowl. Oh, triple ick.

But flushing is a good solution if you go about it correctly. And it can be the perfect solution if you serve a small, elderly or disabled dog·that poops in a controlled indoor area such as a litter box or synthetic grass pan. You can simply use a scooper or toilet paper for pickup. (Tip: Try bokashi mix to keep these indoor poop areas odor-free. See the section on "Bokashi.")

You might also want to try flushable polyvinyl alcohol dog bags that are "hydro-biodegradable." Flushables are

useful for quick pickup and disposal. Just don't expect them to stay intact when transporting DW long distances. The bag begins to come apart when wet.

If the love of your life is a mastiff or a Great Dane, do not dispose of the entire DW clump in a single flush. The bags may be flushable, but none claim to be miraculous. Flushables may disintegrate in the drainpipe en route to the treatment tank, but not in the bowl. The labyrinth of traps, wax rings and closet bends inside residential toilets were never intended to handle mega masses, let alone mega masses compressed in bags. So limit flushable bag loads per common sense and keep your plunger handy.

Never flush bagged or even loose DW into toilets connected to septic tanks. Why? First of all, flushable bags might clog the system. Second, DW contains quite a bit of hair and the bacteria in tanks do not readily digest hair. Hairy residue could obstruct emitters that drain effluent into the soil, requiring the services of your favorite honey dipper.

Do not flush CW under any circumstances as it may contain Toxoplasma gondii, a disease agent affecting marine mammals, pregnant women and people with compromised immune systems.[22] [23]

Want to toilet train your dog? Yes, people do that.

Search "train puppy to use toilet" online for detailed instructions. No, I haven't tried it, so I can contribute nothing remotely helpful. Do not train your cat to go pottie for the reason stated just above.

People who serve multiple dogs can flush safely and efficiently using special systems designed for high-capacity loads. As I mentioned earlier, some animal shelters hose DW directly into sanitary sewers. If flushing large quantities of DW would be a solution for you, find a plumbing professional who can tap into your sanitary sewer and install direct indoor or outdoor access to that line. Be sure to include a lid or other mechanism that will trap sewer odor.

Manufacturers have put some truly inventive systems on the market for DW flushing at high-volume facilities. I won't discuss the features or advisability of these products, but who can resist mentioning names like "Powerloo" and "Whoopsie Away?"

At the other end of the sewer line, flushed DW will be treated and processed in the same way that your local plant handles human waste. Once tested and approved, these biosolids might be buried, landfilled or used as agricultural fertilizer. You can even buy soil amendments made from biosolids for your home turf and garden.

The Milwaukee Metropolitan Sewage District, a pioneer in this field, has been producing and distributing

Milorganite for eighty-five years. These heat-dried pellets are available at garden centers throughout the country. Other treatment facilities have been following Milwaukee's lead, turning biosolids into fertilizer and reducing the need to manufacture chemicals or mine minerals to enrich soil.

Burial

Start up: easy

Learning curve: easy

Maintenance: moderate

Needs: access to fairly spacious private property away from water and edible plants; D/CW container or bag; collection and digging tools

Helpful: moderate physical strength; compostable or paper bags

Advantages: easiest if dogs do their business at burial site; no follow-up actions needed for residue. CW and compostable litter burial is OK.

Disadvantages: frozen ground delays digging; potential scavenger attraction

❦ **End product:** good eco vibes; fertilized, in-place soil

ounds like anyone with a shovel can handle this one. But there's no way to finesse hauling your D/CW to an undisclosed location and ditching it into a shallow grave. You're not Tony Soprano. Pet waste belongs to your pet and, by extension, you. You need a fairly big yard, open land or a willing acquaintance with either of those accommodations to sustain D/CW burial. And remember: a single dog produces around 275 pounds (125 kg) of waste per year.

Select a spot far from sensitive areas such as streams, wetlands, wells, orchards or vegetable gardens to bury D/CW. Stay away from foundations, walls or fences that might be affected by unstable moist soil. Dig your hole or trench at least 8 inches (20 cm) deep so that the waste will not get mixed with topsoil, attract wild animals or be touched by people or pets.

Rather than trench, some people bury D/CW in small, deep holes in soft soil around established ornamental woody plants. Some dig holes like pockets around tree drip lines (the area defined by the outermost circumference of a tree canopy). These practices work in well-tended yards where animals are unlikely to unearth the treasures. When you bury D/CW near plants, be careful not to disturb the roots.

I'm sure you've seen how raw DW deposits burn holes in grass and destroy entire lawns if not cleaned up quickly. Raw D/CW contains ammonia and salt that will damage tender plants directly exposed to these substances. If you bury too much pet waste in shallow holes, you can kill even hardy plants. So bury D/CW sparsely near any orna-mental flora and never use it near tender new plantings.

Do not bury D/CW near edible plants or topdress over them. Parasites with long survival rates might contaminate produce by contact if it falls to the ground. If planting above a burial site, apply a thick layer of clean soil and wait for several months for the waste to degrade. Do not allow new plant roots to immediately touch raw dog waste.

Is raw D/CW instant fertilizer? No. D/CW must have a chance to decompose via microbes and other tiny scavengers in the soil before plant roots can successfully take it up. If you live in a desert or the Arctic Circle with few little critters to work their magic, raw pet waste will languish. But in or on productive soils, raw D/CW will enrich microbial activity and fertility. This is why DW left to rot along hiking trails helps invasive weeds to flourish, ruining original habitats.

Raw D/CW also contains nitrogen, an energy booster for plants. Have you noticed how green circles of grass sometimes surround brown spots on a lawn damaged by DW? The salt and ammonia killed the grass at the center, but the grass at the perimeter enjoyed the mild nitrogen runoff. If you plan to use buried D/CW as plant fertilizer, be sure to let the raw waste decompose so that it is not too strong for application or planting over the burial site. The amount of time needed will depend on climate and soil biology.

I'm not morbid by nature, but when I get questions asking for simple solutions for controlling dog waste at public parks my mind defaults to "burial" and "flowers." I read an article by an enterprising woman who folds recycling DW into her plans for expanding her landscape gardens.

The author starts by excavating the next plot slated for planting flowers, shrubs or trees. Then she disposes of her DW in the garden pit, covering deposits and layering like a pastitsio casserole. When the pit is nearly full, she spreads a generous amount of well-amended soil over the

area and completes her plantings. By the time the roots reach the DW, it has degraded into nice, rich soil.

That woman never revealed her little secret to friends, but swore by the practice and claimed that her garden was the talk of the county. Of course, this and all other tales about the growing power of DW are anecdotal. I can find no formal study on the horticultural benefits of using D/CW as fertilizer. Oh, ick — who would want to be professionally associated with something like that?

Anyway, when I get to thinking about solutions for the tons of DW shunted out of parks in dumpsters, that clever woman always comes to mind. Suppose that a community decided to construct a park and build in a plan for continually using DW as fertilizer for landscaping. Dog People could use shovels available at a do-your-business "pooch patch" and deposit DW into bins. The waste could be used for a garden area right near the site. When one area was covered and planted, another could be started. Every park would be a botanic garden!

This idea could also work for dog breeders, kennels, animal hospitals, shelters and scoopers who want to beautify their sites or provide additional landscaping services. Lots less trash: Smaller Carbon Paw Prints.

I know … grouse, grouse, grouse. Labor intensive. Who has the time? Who would pay for it? Trash trucks (fuel, emissions) and landfills (methane seepage, eventual leaks) are cheaper. So let's leave castles in the sky for another day and return to pet poop on the ground.

If you decide to bury D/CW, do it in productive soil that supports greenery. Do not use plastic bags. Loose D/CW is best, or use paper or certified compostable bags, both of which will eventually decompose. Breaking open the bags or simply not closing them will speed up the process considerably. You may want to add compost, leaves, shredded paper, wood chips or bokashi to the waste to aid degradation.

In cold climates, the ground can freeze solid, limiting your activity. If you want to keep burial going year round, dig your pit during the warm season and leave plenty of loose soil and leaves nearby for topping off.

One more bit of advice. If you have a spouse or partner, be sure the neighbors see you together on a regular basis so all of that digging doesn't draw suspicion.

Biodigestion / septic bin

Start up: moderate

Learning curve: moderate

Maintenance: easy

Needs: access to private property away from foundations, walls, water and edible plants; well-drained soil; DW container or bag; digging and collection tools; deep hole

Helpful: specially prepared in-ground bin with lid; septic starter; mild winters or winters with thaws

Advantages: easiest if dogs do business in yard; system tolerates neglect

Disadvantages: process stops below 40°F (4°C) but restarts in warmer weather; methane emission and possible odors. Do not digest and drain CW!

End product: good eco vibes; fertilized soil if you choose not to harvest; fertilizer residue for ornamental plants if you choose to harvest

Doggie septic bins (biodigesters) are often termed "composters," but these systems really degrade DW by a process very different from composting. Composting is aerobic — powered for the most part by tiny critters that thrive on oxygen. Microbes that decompose material in a septic bin are anaerobic. They do their work

— biodigestion — in dark, airless places, where they emit methane. Good composting is odorless. Biodigestion that is totally odorless just isn't working. But the odor can be very easily controlled.

Cityfarmer.org (Canada's Office of Urban Agriculture) offers step-by-step guides and videos for preparing these disposal units.[24] Here is the most commonly used method.

1. Locate an area on your property with well-drained soil and a low water table, away from water sources and home foundations. You can check soil drainage by throwing a bucket of water into the hole. If it drains into the soil, good. If not, consider another site. If you have a well make sure your system is not within about 90 feet (25 meters) of the head since that's your seepage radius (it will be a little farther on the uphill side).

2. Find an old plastic garbage can. Drill a dozen or so drainage holes in the sides and cut out the bottom entirely. A keyhole saw works great.

3. Dig a deep hole, deep enough to bury the can. Below the local frost line, microbes will do their work longer as surface temperatures drop.

4. Toss some rocks or gravel into the hole for drainage, positioning the can so it sits a little higher than the soil level.

5. Place the lid on top. You might want to paint it with something clever like "dog waste bin."

Now you're ready to start scooping DW into your tank. Each week sprinkle in some water and inexpensive septic starter, which is available at hardware stores. The starter is a non-caustic powder that promotes natural bacterial growth. Bokashi also works as a starter (see the following section). The DW will degrade, shrink in mass, enter into the subsoil and leave a residue.

If you don't want to build your own tank, there are several commercially manufactured in-ground systems that also allow DW to leach into the ground. Some have decorative tops, which will fit in with a more finished, manicured landscape. The manuals warn that these system might not work under various soil, climate or water table conditions, so consider carefully before investing.

Do these DW septic systems fill up? The digesting bacteria drastically reduce bulk. But it's conceivable that they might top out, especially with a lot of DW input. When a septic bin fills, you have a choice.

- Harvest the resulting residue as nonedible garden fertilizer. Remember, this stuff is the equivalent of sewage sludge — dank material that might contain bacteria, viruses and small parasitic worms. Handle and use with care.

- Simply pull up the can, shovel dirt over the contents and start over. You might want to plant a nice butterfly bush over the spot — just don't plant the roots directly into raw residue. If you cover it over with lawn, the grass will always be greener over the DW.

Not fussy? Just dig a hole. Cityfarmer.org features a video of Sharon and her little dog Nellie. For ten years, Sharon has been tossing Nellie's DW into the same deep hole under her outdoor stairway. The hole is neatly topped with a wood frame and lid. Sharon adds starter and water to the hole from time to time, but that's about it. No odors, no problems. When the hole fills, she plans to harvest the residue and bury it among her ornamental plants. Sharon has been successfully biodigesting DW this way for twenty-five years!

Please be forewarned. Septic processing stops when the thermometer drops below 40°F (4°C). When this happens the DW will stop shrinking, so be sure that your bin is big enough to get you through cold spells or have a backup plan. Odors can be a bigger problem in warmer climates, but they can usually be resolved by adding additional septic starter and water.

All of these little inconveniences are insignificant when you consider this: if you biodigest your pet's waste, you'll be part of a much bigger resource diversion and recovery

movement. Biodigestion doesn't just upcycle organics into fertile soil — it also generates methane gas that can be purified into natural gas or used to turn turbines that produce electricity. William Brinton, president of Woods End Laboratories in Mount Vernon, Maine, estimates that harnessing the power of one ton of animal waste could produce 50 gallons (190 liters) worth of diesel-equivalent energy — enough to power a house in New England for two weeks![5]

Bokashi (Essential Microorganisms/EM)

Start up: moderate

Learning curve: moderate or demanding depending on interest/system

Maintenance: moderate or demanding depending on interest/system

Needs: bokashi mixture including essential/effective microorganisms (EM), wheat bran (or other carbon source), molasses (or other sugar source); end use for finished soil enhancements.

Helpful: airtight containers or bag; diligence to follow instructions; conscientious management skills

Advantages: fast; negligible methane emissions; virtually odorless; ideal for apartments and other small dwellings; highly scalable to space and amount of waste; degrades any organics; works indoors or out; mix has many upcycling, household, health and gardening uses

Disadvantages: need to either blend bokashi mixture in advance or order relatively expensive premixed products

End product: good eco vibes, enriched solid residue and tea for ornamentals

D on't let the exotic name intimidate you. If you think that bokashi involves mysterious brews, cosmic mindsets and tinkling temple wind chimes, you are channeling kung fu. Bokashi is not complicated and the learning curve is fairly short. It is simply anaerobic digestion "on steroids." The process is fast and mildly acidic, similar to pickling and fermentation rather than rotting.

Bokashi started long ago in the Far East as a natural farming philosophy. Over many generations, advocates cultivated local organisms that would quickly degrade organic waste into high-quality fertilizer. While modern

Toronto's green bin program

Large-scale biodigesters that process organic waste are expensive propositions costing hundreds of thousands of dollars. Prosperous farm operations install units that degrade animal waste and generate electricity, avoiding manure lagoons that require dedicated acreage and pose potential threats to clean water. Environmental grants are often available for install-ing these systems in an effort to prevent water pollution.

The vast majority of US municipalities offer only one disposal option for pet waste: landfills. But the City of Toronto is aiming at 70 percent residential waste diversion. One component of its plan is its Green Bin Program, a system that accepts all organics — including the dreaded pet waste and disposable diapers.

practitioners have adapted the process to enhance household upcycling, many of the original wild cultured microorganisms (OM) are the same used today, as essential microorganisms (EM).

Bokashi is sometimes called "bokashi composting," just as septic bins are loosely termed "composters." The word "compost" is used because the resulting residue looks like compost and is a soil amendment meant to be used sparingly, like compost. But both biodigestion and bokashi are anaerobic processes that involve sealing out air, whereas composting requires air flow.

Collected materials are sent through a hydropulper, which spins them into liquid pulp while separating out plastic bags and other nonorganic residue. The pulp moves on to a huge tank where it is digested by microorganisms in just twenty days. The result is a digestate that resembles gingerbread dough and biogas — a renewable energy source.

The digestate is used as a "starter" for composting municipal yard waste. This process uses air, heat and light to foster bacteria and fungi that eliminate pathogens and produces compost that doesn't smell and can be used safely to enrich soil. The city plans to use the biogas — a mixture of methane and carbon dioxide — as a power source.[25]

Lime, leaves or sawdust stimulate the decomposition of buried material. Septic starter revs up biodigestion. When it comes to bokashi, grains that have been steeped in a sugary solution are the energy booster of choice. These ingredients are thoroughly blended with EM and stored in an airtight container. The result is a spongy, fragrant bokashi mixture that can be sprinkled throughout organic material to kick-start degradation. After a couple of weeks sealed tightly with this heavenly grain-sugar hash, the essential microorganisms are supercharged and ready to tear into organic waste like so many mesophilic piranhas.

The Park Spark Project

A much smaller temporary project using a methane digester charmed visitors at a Cambridge, Massachusetts, dog park a few years back. Park Spark was a temporary art installation that invited the public to deposit DW into a colorful enclosed tank and stir the contents using an external wheel.

Sure, we've been warned never to stir this stuff. But mixing gave the bacteria in the digestion tank better access to their "food," which sped up the biomagic. Methane gas produced in the process collected inside the top of the tank and was piped to an old-fashioned gas lamp that softly lit the park.

Besides providing an ambience rarely offered at dog parks, Park Spark demonstrated a simple green technology that turns methane (CH_4), a highly potent greenhouse gas, into the tamer carbon dioxide

Practitioners can purchase prepared bokashi mix or create their own blends. The uber microorganisms in bokashi mix will devour anything that once lived, including leftover fruits, vegetables, cheese, meat, hair, bones, your extracted appendix and, yes, D/CW. These guys are not picky. Just give them an airless hangout and they will break down any organic material into carbon, nitrogen, phosphorus, potassium and essential biology — components that rejuvenate soil and are readily accessible to plant roots.

Unlike simple rotting or slow biodigestion, the

(CO^2) and water. The project also questioned our everyday assumptions about trashing waste and proved that everything — even DW — has a useful purpose. Park Spark inspired the city of Gilbert, Arizona, and Arizona State University students to power up their E-TURD (Energy Transformation Using Reactive Digestion) program — a gas-burning light at Cosmo Dog Park fueled by a dog waste digester.[26]

The Pacific Shellfish Institute in Olympia, Washington is also investigating the possibilities of using poo power to divert dog waste runoff from Puget Sound.[27] Their research references another recent study finding that dog waste might actually enhance biogas production of field grass by breaking down the molecular structure, allowing anaerobes to digest it.[28] The city of Surrey, British Columbia, is factoring biodigestion and composting into its long-range plans for sustainable dog park maintenance.[29]

microbial action of bokashi does not produce greenhouse gases that attract bugs and other scavengers. When properly managed, the process is practically odorless, leaving only a slight pickle or cider vinegar scent.

Those are the flat-out basics of bokashi. Devotees of this practice are fascinated with the endless variations of mixtures and techniques. explore the dynamics, let's look at simple approaches for Dog or Cat People who want to cut to the chase and enjoy the benefits without a lot of fuss.

Bokashi lite...
Moderate learning curve and systems

Let's say you don't have the time or interest for DIY but still want a quick, odorless, space-saving practice. In that case, you might want to search online for a commercial product that makes it easy. Prefab containers with their premixed cultures — usually EM-inoculated bagged grains — are fairly pricey, so consider your specific needs and return on investment.

One big advantage of commercial kits is that they provide step-by-step instructions that will keep you out of trouble and get the job done. There are product lines tailored for using bokashi to upcycle DW. One company offers a special pet-waste accelerant concentrate and another features a mixture called "Dookashi." One highly promoted system for odorless, submerged fermenting features two attractive, stackable, three-and-a-half-gallon plastic buckets. You simply deposit DW into the top bucket while the one on the bottom completes the cycle. According to the company video, 30 pounds (14 kilos) of DW can be finished in a single week, so it would take an average dog more than a month to fill a bucket. The bottom bucket needs to "rest" for only a week before it is finished and ready to dump and bury as a fertilizer for nonedible plants.

A commercial dry method provides an airtight container that looks for all the world like a portable beverage dispenser. You simply pop in a fitted screen trap, layer chopped up scraps and blend them with prescribed amounts of the packaged bokashi mix. A spigot at the bottom makes it easy to tap out the "tea," which mixes 1:100 with water to produce a fertilizer. (Spoiler alert: tea can be a bit stinky.)

Of course, the finished bokashi residue — odorless, degraded material or sludge — doesn't simply disappear into thin air. You need to bury it according to guidelines in order to enrich soil. If the ground is frozen, you will have to store it until the soil is workable.

Before purchasing a commercial bokashi system, talk

to a distributor about whether it can be successfully used for D/CW. If he convinces you that it will work, be sure that you receive clear instructions so that you can adapt the system to your specific purpose. If it does not work as described, contact the company immediately to trouble-shoot the process.

Bokashi nitty-gritty ...
Moderate to demanding learning curve and systems

Do you suspect that the system manufacturers are just trying to sell you molded plastic containers and hook you on expensive measured and branded mixtures? Are you an economy-minded self-starter who's ready to find out if a DIY bokashi system will work for you? Are you long on good intentions but short on cash? Use the easy bokashi mix recipe on page 104.

Below are three simple methods that just require some time and effort but little investment. Keep in mind that bokashi is like cooking; once you get the basics down, variations are as endless as your creativity. Just keep your D/CW bokashi system separate from other waste unless you intend to use the residue for nonedibles only.

1. "Bokashi soup"/submerge method (indoors or out): Fill an airtight container to the half-mark with water containing bokashi mixture. Add waste. Cover and repeat. When the container is almost full, stop adding waste and wait for the degradation to finish. Pour residual fermented waste water — now fertilizer — into a hole, mix with soil and cover with additional soil. Wait for several months before using this as planting soil, as the bokashi residue may be too strong for root development and uptake.

2. "Bokashi stew"/dry method (indoors or out): Fill an airtight container with a layer of waste mingled with bokashi mix. Cover and repeat until full. Stop adding waste and wait for cycle completion. Use finished solid and leachate residue as fertilizer. Or siphon off the leachate (tea), dilute it with water (1:100) and use it as a liquid fertilizer or spray.

3. "Bokashi lasagna" (outdoors): Place any container with an open bottom or make an enclosure on bare ground. Add a layer of waste and mingle with bokashi mix. Add 2–3 inches (5–8 cm) of dirt. Cover and repeat until full. Stop adding waste and wait for cycle completion. Rest the residue before using it as fertilizer.

Sounds kind of easy, huh? But many a beginner with good intentions has ended up with unintended consequences (stinky slime, no progress). If this happens, you have two choices: 1) surrender or 2) figure it out, Sherlock.

If you pick choice #1, maybe you weren't cut out for this bokashi thing after all. If you pick #2, congratulations — you've just grabbed your ticket for a cool adventure in bokashi upcycling!

Just add a little more bokashi mixture, mix it up and move it to a warmer spot. Do some experimenting and online troubleshooting. Like composting, bokashi can be very forgiving. You will succeed, Grasshopper!

You could say bokashi is the anti-21st-century, senses-pulverizing, action-movie gig. It is a subtle process requiring patience, sensory interface and careful observation. Does it look right? Is it starting to smell "off?" How can I tweak the process? Once you get your system down for D/CW or any organic — OmmmmMG — you are rewarded with a quick, odorless and entirely satisfying process.

Bokashi involves few rules and a great deal of trial and error, self-expression and information-sharing. For instance, in the basic methods above, I refer to the residues as "fertilizer," but mixing the finished product directly with soil to nourish your garden is just one option. You can team up bokashi mix or residue with other pet-waste upcycling processes: as a starter in your biodigester/septic tank or D/CW burial, as an accelerator in your compost pile or to improve the menu at your worm farm. (I had my own aha moment while writing this section. I successfully introduced bokashi into my own household upcycling system. See "My EM-piphany" under "Adapting composting to space and climate" below.)

You can put partially finished bokashi waste in the bottom of a flower pot, cover it with potting soil and add your favorite houseplant. The residue will finish decomposing and the plant will thrive as its roots reach for the loot at the bottom of the pot. You can also trickle down nutrients by adding diluted tea when watering plants.

D/CW bokashi residue is definitely NOT to be used for growing edibles, but you can bury the granular bokashi mixture itself anywhere you garden. Mix it with soil when planting to nurture new fruits, herbs or vegetables. Blend it with potting soil in containers. Use EM "straight" to eliminate algae in your pond or birdbath and to sanitize your swimming pool.

The bokashi mix is a natural biology accelerator and odor controller, so it has more household uses than vinegar. Dilute it in water and use it as a septic sanitizer and drain cleaner. Sprinkle it with kitty litter or animal bedding. Or sprinkle it on your cereal. Clean bokashi mix can work as a probiotic for you and your pet. No lie.

Bokashi mix recipes and information on many, many other purposes are available online. Combining grains,

EM, water and molasses to rustle up a batch of DIY bokashi smells fresh and yeast-y — like mixing up enough
biscuit dough to feed a platoon. With a little nosing
around, you will find uses for bokashi that simplify your
life and, it would seem, significantly reduce the number
of items in your grocery cart.

General bokashi alert: Whether you go with a purchased kit or cobble your own system together, cold
weather can put a temporary kybosh on your D/CW
bokashi operation. You can ferment indoors — minimum
40°F (4°C), optimum 70–100°F (21–38°C) — but you
will need to eventually work a good bit of the residue into
workable soil. So if you want the process to continue in a
timely manner, prepare a storage system that allows your
project to function during a hard freeze.

Composting

Start up: easy or moderate, depending on complexity
of enclosure
Learning curve: moderate
Maintenance: easy, moderate or demanding,
depending on ambition and dedication
Needs: Carbon ("brown") waste source; access to private property; end use for finished soil enhancements;
digging/turning tools

Helpful: moderate physical strength; enclosure; tumbler
Advantages: easiest if dogs do business in yard; odorless if done correctly; fragrance "high"; emits carbon dioxide — a greenhouse gas much less potent than methane
Disadvantages: process stops outdoors below 40°F (4°C); potential scavenger attraction
End products: finished compost for nonedible plants; good eco vibes (upcycling D/CW plus using compost reduces water waste and improves soil structure)

Composting is the perfect technique for cheap, chronic slackers who nonetheless (love the word) enjoy getting physically involved with the sight, feel and smell of what they are doing. That might describe dogs ... or people like me. Composting trundles along with you or without you. You can space it out for months without guilt and then get the process humming along again.

You don't need a lot of money to compost. In fact, our frugal forebears perfected the practice as a way to avoid the cost and effort of moving waste while generating a freebie crop booster. Composting is very forgiving. If you goof up, you can get back on track fast. When the compost heap freezes, it will perk back into action as temperatures rise. You can speed it up or slow it down. Thermophilic hotshot microbes and their mesophilic

friends do all the work with little effort on your part.

I suspect I might be hooked on the delicious scents of diverse microorganisms that live in compost pile and, in fact, all good dirt. These critters release fumes that boost levels of serotonin and norepinephrine like a mind-altering drug. Scientists call it "geosmin," the same chemical feast that gives vegetables that grow underground their succulent earthy taste. It's hard to turn compost on a warm day without feeling happy.

Composting is not rocket science. But composting that involves D/CW should not be approached in the same frivolous way as composting food scraps or yard waste. We will discuss the differences later. For now, here's a quick overview of the process.

- Casual composters simply throw what's handy into the heap.
- Start with a balance of "green" nitrogen-rich materials (grass clippings, fruit and veggie peels, coffee grounds) and carbon-rich "browns" (autumn leaves, paper, straw or sawdust). Organisms that decompose organic matter use carbon (C) as a source of energy and nitrogen (N) for building cell structure, while the dry carbon material bulks up the "green" and keeps air flowing.
- A nice C/N ratio for food scraps is 3/C to 1/N. For raw manure (N), a good ratio is around 30/C to 1/N.

- Never use pressure-treated/composite chips or saw-dust, which contain arsenic and chromium. Do not add grass clippings or weeds that have been treated with insecticides or herbicides. Keep seeding weeds out of the mix.

- Rough up the soil that will be a base for your compost pile. This will help open the door for microorganisms in the soil, so they can move on up and help with degradation.

- Heap the materials on an area at least three feet (one meter) long by three feet (one meter) wide by three feet (one meter) high. Your pile will grow as you add material. Maintain a rounded shape with the top a bit flattened.

- Keep the pile relatively moist with circulating air. The pile heats up at the center, then cools down as "hot" microbes cycle through their feeding frenzy. During the cool cycles, other organisms continue to degrade complex organic compounds to produce humus-like substances.

- Turning the pile occasionally will speed up the process under certain circumstances, but is not necessary. More important is using textured "brown" material like hay and straw to create pockets of air and making sure the pile has the right moisture content.

- If the climate is dry, cover the top of the pile with a piece of carpet that will keep moisture in but allow the microorganisms to breathe. You might need to cover with a tarp or other waterproof material in a wetter climate or during downpours.

- Keep layering the pile with some "brown" and then "green" material.

- When the pile looks big-enough-to-you (this is all so personal!), stop adding to it and start a new one.

- Compost should be "aged/cured/seasoned" — essentially, rested — so that it is mild enough for plants. "Finished" compost is dark and soil-like, crumbles to the touch, smells rich and has few identifiable pieces of the original materials that fed the pile.

- Uncured compost can produce phytotoxins harmful to plants. DIY D/CW compost should be cured for a year before using.

Many community organizations offer excellent composting classes — yes, even D/CW composting

Thermophilic microbes

According to one theory, thermophiles may be our "universal ancestor," creatures that developed 3.6 billion years ago during intense primordial heat. In spite of the fact that they need a hot environment to thrive, they are literally everywhere, just waiting in a sound sleep until

classes. Compost pet waste as you would a "green" material, either in separate piles or with your other organics if you don't plan to use the compost on edible plantings. When composting D/CW, deposit this waste in the "hot spot" at the upper middle part of the pile. Take extra precautions for cleanliness and keep in mind that you are working with a material that presents the same potential complications as any other nontraditional "green" organic additive (see Composting "no-no's" below).

Search online for your local USDA Cooperative Extension office to access the best information on composting in your area. You'll also find tips on troubleshooting if your compost pile smells "off," smolders, attracts flies or simply sits there looking pitiful. (What is it, Lassie? Pile too small? Too dry? What is it, girl?)

Feeling motivated? You can construct compost enclosures with proper ventilation using non-pressure-treated/ non-composite lumber, old wooden pallets, cinder blocks or chicken wire. But scraping an area of ground and piling on materials in layers also works just fine.

condition are right for them to recreate the ancient heat they love. If we help them by creating a compost heap, they reward us by turning our rotten castoffs into life-sustaining soil. Makes composting seem kind of majestic, doesn't it?

Composting "no-no's"

If you have children, dogs or wildlife about, always screen off access to any compost heap that contains non-vegetable matter such as breads, meats, oils, dairy and, yes, D/CW. These traditional composting no-no's will eventually degrade like everything else in the heap, but may tip the "green"/nitrogen balance too far, smell as a result of anaerobic digestion, develop mold, attract scavengers or require additional time for degradation. These potential problems will morph into reality if a "no-no-heavy" compost pile is not tended with due diligence

So composting D/CW is OK. Just be sure to follow directions from a reputable source. And there's no more reputable source than the US Department of Agriculture (USDA).

DW composting came into its own as a plausible and serious undertaking in 2005, when the USDA Natural Resources Conservation Service in Alaska published "Dog Waste Composting." (These brave researchers went above and beyond "Oh, ick!") The report is based on an earlier study conducted by the Fairbanks Soil and Water Conservation at a local sled dog yard, plus more than a decade of additional experience. Authoritative evidence in this document shows how careful DW composting can reduce water pollution and fertilize soil while saving time, money, energy and landfill space.[30]

For step-by-step instructions on how to compost DW, go to "USDA: Dog Waste Composting," posted online. The report is also a helpful resource on cold-weather composting, supplies, bin designs and minimizing health risks. However it does not guarantee that compost processed according to instructions will be free of pathogens and recommends using it on nonedible plantings.

Furiously turning any compost pile to "heat up all parts" is unnecessary and may even be detrimental. The heat generated by thermophiles is not the only thing that kills harmful pathogens; other microorganisms that kick into the process produce antibiotics that destroy the bad critters. Those same natural antibiotics remain in the compost to suppress plant diseases and attract worms. Aging D/CW compost for a year will invite a diversity of beneficial microorganisms, bugs and earthworms to further sanitize and mellow the material.

As with all the DIY upcycling practices in this book, no matter how carefully you monitor your processes, do not use compost that includes D/CW on or near edible plantings. Like human waste, D/CW is a biosolid. Composted biosolids must meet EPA standards for pathogen mitigation before being used for agricultural applications.

General composting alert: Composting comes to a screeching halt when temperatures dip below 40°F (4°C).

Be sure you have a storage system for waste and unfinished compost to get you through prolonged cold weather.

Adapting dog/cat waste composting to space and climate

I'm not in Pittsburgh anymore. No more rainy Eastern days, organic-rich topsoil, lush greenery. No ubiquitous raccoons and rats, just the occasional coyote. The "back forty" near the stream belongs to someone else, along with the ill-advised DW burial grounds. I had to consider my new circumstances, how much time and effort I wanted to put into keeping pet waste out of the trash, and how that project could dovetail with my other household organics recycling.

We moved to a tightly built suburban subdivision on a high arid plain in Aurora, Colorado. We have sand and clay dirt with no direct drainage into a natural water source. We never had the heart to replace Gretchen with an ordinary dog. But we continue to adopt shelter cats whose eyes meet ours with a proper mix of cockiness and longing. Our latest is a spunky tuxedo cat named Max, my poster child for the section on small-animal bedding litter.

My new dilemma: how to upcycle combined household organic material for two people and a cat in a 6-foot-by-12-foot (2-meter-by-4-meter) strip of barren yard between our house and a 6-foot (2-meter) fence that is much too close to a neighbor's back porch. The strip was covered with fabric and river stones, common ground prep for unplanted areas in our community.

A combination of biodigestion and composting was originally the best way I'd found to process our waste, given the circumstances. I have no real schedule. All waste materials shrink around 50 percent while processing, but the rate depends on temperatures, humidity and type of additives. In my Rube Goldberg setup, I simply empty various containers when they are full and shift contents up the line to the next process step.

Super scientific holding-area-is-full-so-dump-it method

1. Storage and digestion. I tear up vegetable waste (fruit and vegetable cuttings, leftovers, coffee grounds in filters) and freeze it in a heavy recycled plastic bag. I trash meat, bones and oil but slip moldy cheese in with the compostables without repercussions. When the bag is full, I dump the frozen chunk into a lidded plastic cat litter bucket, a remnant of Max's clay litter days. Freezer bag full = move contents to outdoor waste bucket I line up and sequentially fill six buckets so that the

oldest waste is closest to my composting trench. When a bucket is full of rotted/digested waste and leachate, it is ready to fuel compost. Even in warm weather, these buckets attract only a few tiny flying bugs and do not smell bad until the lid is lifted — then yucko! Waste bucket full = dump in trench if trench has room for more waste

2. Trench composting. I wouldn't have chosen to use a trench if I were still in western Pennsylvania. But the system works fine in Aurora, where we get very little rain and the surrounding dirt is porous sand. Because of the dryness and good, safe drainage, exposure to air at the top only and occasional turning is enough to support composting. And the material sets below the frost line, so the microbes turn slacker but keep doing their degradation thing unless we get a long, hard freeze.

To get this process started, I dug a 5-foot-by-1½-foot (150-by-50-cm) open trench, about 1½ feet (50 cm) deep, in the center of the strip. I eventually want to restore the area, so I rolled back the fabric on long poles that run along each side of the trench and saved the sand in some of my many, many surplus litter buckets. I started composting with just food scraps ("green"), crushed dry leaves ("brown") and sand ("unavoidable"). The hotshot thermophilic microbes showed up like a kitty on a clean basket of laundry and started doing what they do best.

Now that these thermophiles have fired up the material, I have an active mass that continually starts composting additional waste. I add more rotted waste only if more than half of the material in the trench has a moderately dry compost appearance. More about my "evolving 'brown' material" shortly.

When I am ready to empty a bucket, I dig a hole in the compost at one end of the trench and dump the oldest, moldiest sludge. I do not do this evenings, Saturdays, Sundays or holidays when our next-door neighbors might be home. I also delay dumping on Thursdays, neighbor-mom's day off, because, lifting the lids and dumping the sludgy buckets of digesting food scraps are the only parts of the process that really stink.

But the smell quickly dissipates when the stuff is covered over with dry compost already in the trench. Dumping this food scrap slurry is a bit like throwing slop to the hogs, except the hogs are microscopic and don't snort and knock you over when they're excited.

3. Adding CW and litter to the mix. About that "evolving 'brown' material." I can always use our leaves as a "brown" bulking material, but what I really need to

reduce is our cat's carbon paw print. When it's time to empty a bag of Max's CW and used litter, I dig a hole in the trench compost, drop in the litter and mix it up with the compost.

If the timing is right, I dump another bucket of sloppy food-scrap waste over the litter and cover it all up. The dry sawdust absorbs food scrap leachate and, along with used and shredded paper towels and Kleenex, provides all the "brown" component needed to bulk up the "green" food scraps and CW. The carbon also energizes the composting process. (I take the leaves and grass clippings to use as mulch at a local school garden.) Cat litter bag full = mix with trench compost

4. Resting in the trench. Every time I make a deposit, and occasionally in between times, I turn the part of the compost that is mostly fragrant and fluffy ... or on its way. At a good stopping point, I stop contributing and simply turn and rest the compost for a week or so. Just let it be!

5. Tumbler composting. By the time the latest batch of in-ground compost looks like rich soil with just a few unfinished pieces and has the lovely scent of jazzed-up microorganisms, the trench is fluffy and full. So it's time to shovel as much of it as possible into my 30-by-22-inch (75-by-55-cm) barrel tumbler to finish

the composting process. Trench full of nice compost = move material into tumbler.

Leave the material in the tumbler for at least a month, turning occasionally. Check out the tumbler contents. The earthy smell, texture and coolness of the material tells me it's ready to cure. At that point, empty the tumbler contents into clean cat litter buckets, close the lid and let it cogitate until you have time to amend the soil in your container or landscape plantings. Tumbler full of finished material = move it into clean buckets to age before using as soil amendment.

Temperature dips, troubleshooting, elbow grease and rewards

Think of the microbiotic processes going on in the buckets, trench and tumbler in terms of rotations per minute (rpm). Car engines typically operate at around 2,000–3,000 rpm when cruising and idle at around 750–900 rpm. But they can reach much higher rotations. Formula One cars are limited to 18,000 rpm. In high summer, I'm keeping up with the Grand Prix but when temperatures drop as the season changes, my system idles and stalls. The material in the buckets and the tumbler freezes. I add more storage buckets. Incredibly, the process

then revs up again during the next warm spell.

My bucket brigade system slows down as winter approaches. Luckily it never freezes for long here in Colorado, where chances are good the UPS driver will be delivering Christmas bundles in shorts. During warm months, when we generate more fresh vegetable and fruit scraps, including melon rinds, I empty the frozen bag into an outdoor bucket nearly every day. That dumping slows down to three times a week in winter when coffee grounds are the biggest contribution.

I turn the trench compost and spin the tumbler from time to time so that the aerobic microbes get the air they need to stay productive. If there is too much dampness, anaerobic microbes will begin to dominate and the material will begin to digest instead of compost. The material gets mucky and might exude a septic tank/methane odor.

But composting is (here are those words again) very forgiving. Throw in some brown/carbon, fluff it up and

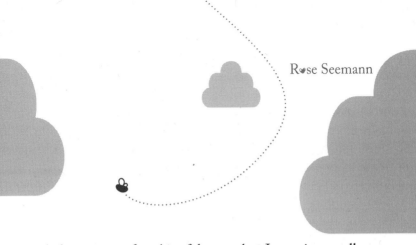

bide your time for a bit of dry weather. In no time at all the aerobic critter cavalry will charge in to the rescue.

On paper my system might seem like a lot of work. But once any enterprise moves from trial and error to effectiveness to efficiency to habit, it's easy. Like a new baby, it just snuggles neatly into your everyday tasks.

I bury a full bag of used cat litter in the trench every week in all weather. I dump the digested material in the waste buckets twice a week in warm weather, and once a month or less when temperatures keep it cold. I move all of the material through the system and fertilize my plants three to four times a year. I don't turn the material when it's cold. I hibernate with the little critters. Like farming, composting fine-tunes your spirit to nature because you need to calibrate your daily activities to the seasons, temperatures and weather.

Sure, my Rube Goldberg system requires some effort. If my community provided organics recycling, I would run out tomorrow to pick up my green bin. But the effort is not much greater than pitching organics in a trashcan, dealing with lingering kitchen garbage odors, double bagging and hauling heavy loads to the curb. I like to think of it as weight-bearing exercise without the athletic club membership fees.

And the resulting kitchen-scrap-cat-litter compost is more than a bonus! It has transformed the 100-percent sand and clay border around our lawn into amended soil that nurtures a lavish riot of perennial flowers, shrubs and trees. And we have worms — actual garden worms — right here on a high arid plain. This transformation was accomplished without bagged soils, retail compost or commercial fertilizer. Throw in the compost highs and good eco vibes and there's no going back!

With a little consideration, any Dog or Cat Person can come up with an upcycling practice, or combination of practices, that will work in their climate for their household and their pets. Once you find a good system, keep tweaking until it is a great system.

Combining practices (tweaking): my EM-piphany

What do essential microorganisms have to do with my hyperadapted composting system?

As I wrapped up the "Bokashi" section in this book, it hit me. What if I use a bokashi mix to ferment the bucket waste instead of letting it rot and stink au naturel? After all, getting a reputation as a neighborhood pariah was a real concern.

I gave it the old hard-knocks try and ordered a "month's supply" (2.2 lb/1 kg) of premixed bokashi online. A clear plastic resealable bag arrived filled with wonderfully fragrant brown bran. I explained the mysterious package to Chuck, who replied, "Oh, good. I thought you were going to feed it to me."

The bokashi was delivered on Thursday, my neighbor's day off. And she was enjoying that beautiful June day. Laundry flapped on a porch clothesline and the sliding door to her kitchen was wide open. I decided to delay the experiment. Covert activities involving funny smells would blow my cover. Hopefully the bokashi would change all that.

The coast was clear the next day, so I visited the buckets with my bag of bokashi. A dozen or so tiny flies (as kids we called them "no-see-ems") swirled around the lids waiting for landing instructions. I opened the bucket filled with the oldest food scraps, which had probably been sitting there for weeks. The vomit-like odor was overpowering. Yuck.

I threw in a handful of bokashi mix and mixed it in with a stick. I did the same with each bucket, oldest material to newest. Each reeked with varying degrees of disgust.

So what do you think happened? Cynical as a crow but secretly hopeful, I let the bokashi work over the weekend. On Monday morning I noticed that the flies were gone. I checked the contents of the buckets gingerly. The newer food scraps were still intact but a bit zombified and had a pickly pungent smell. The decomposed food scraps and slurry had just a whiff of an off smell, but not nearly as bad as on Friday. Essentially, the overwhelming odor in the buckets was gone.

The bokashi worked! I was "brewing" the food scraps instead of rotting them, which felt ever so much more proficient. And ... the bokashi-brewed sludge composted fast! Onion skins, banana peels, lettuces, melon rind cubes — the whole potpourri of putrescibles that I buried and turned in the ditch — were unrecognizable in days instead of weeks. The CW and litter thrown into the ditch directly from its bag also degraded faster, simply through secondhand contact.

Right away I knew I would need a lot of this bokashi stuff to deodorize and speed up digestion in the buckets and accelerate composting in both the trench and the tumbler. Also, why not start degrading the CW and litter right in the bag? Or even in the litter box? Now

all I needed to do was find a way to whip up whopping quantities of DIY bokashi that would not set me back ten dollars a pound. Easy!

Start with a simple mixture requiring just EM, molasses, bran and water. Search online for "EM bokashi recipes" or use this simple one.

10 lb. of bokashi mix	10 cups water
4 tbsp. EM-1	10 lb. bran
4 tbsp. molasses	

You can buy a bottle of EM-1 online; purchase the molasses at the grocery store and a 40-pound bag of bran at a local feed supply store. The ingredients are inexpensive considering the bulk supply of bokashi they provide. I started by mixing five pounds of bokashi by hand in a clean cat litter bucket. It was fun. Kids especially would get a kick out of working this spongy material that smells like muffin dough.

I fermented the mixture in a tightly closed plastic bag, kept it in a lidded container for a month and voila — nice bokashi! Based on my initial purchase, I figured I would go through around one-and-a-half pounds a month. Since fermented bokashi needs to be air-dried for a few hours on a tarp before long-term storage, I would be sure to rustle up enough to get me through the windy spring season.

Now that bokashi has given my formerly smelly system a professional edge, I am an upcycling aficionado instead of a litter bucket klutz. I even hung some temple wind chimes in a nearby tree. My neighbor doesn't seem to mind and, I must say, they add a nice touch.

Moldering

Start up: moderate if outdoor space is limited OR easy if isolated outdoor space is adequate

Learning curve: moderate

Maintenance: easy

Needs: dry sawdust; waterproof containers with tight lids, nylon netting, screening, duct tape, bungee cord or tie; end use for finished soil enhancement

Helpful: compost crank; patience

Advantages: minimal maintenance

Disadvantages: long waiting time

End Products: good eco vibes; rich soil enhancement

Definitions for "moldering" include:

* slowly decaying or disintegrating, esp. because of neglect;
* left somewhere and not used or cared for.

"Neglect ... not cared for" — these words make moldering D/CW an eco-sensitive couch potato's dream.

Moldering is sometimes referred to as "cold composting" or "slow composting." Essentially, you do very little and degrading critters do it all. The process requires only natural air circulation and moseys along below mammalian body temperatures — 40°F (4°C) to 98°F (37°C). Decomposition is suspended below 40°F (4°C), but picks up again when temperatures rise.

Here is easy way to molder C/DW. It does not require much space but should be done in a spot with little foot traffic, so that your project will not raise comments or criticism from people who mean well but wouldn't "get it." You will want to keep prolonged rain and snow off your operation, so it should be either 1) located under a structure (porch, deck, lean-to) or 2) covered with container lids, a tarp or a piece of plexiglass, corrugated metal or any other handy sheeting material during precipitation (at all other times the screen at the top of the buckets should remain open to allow air circulation).

You will need several plastic buckets with tight lids. The number and size of these buckets will depend on your number of pets. If you have one to three cats or dogs, you can start a single ten-gallon heavy-duty plastic can and add others as needed. If you have a dog daycare business serving 50 pets per day, 55-gallon plastic drums might be in order. The goal is to degrade

D/CW slowly by exposing the mass to air while using non-pressure-treated/non-composite sawdust to bulk the material and control odor.

- Cut a hole 2 inches (5 cm) across in the side of the bucket and then cut out a piece of window screen large enough to cover the hole. Use duct tape all around to attach the screen over the hole inside the bucket. This will keep flies out. (Moldering is not a particularly smelly process, but flies are sensitive "sniffers." Luckily they give up and get busy looking for better prospects if access is denied.)
- Suspend a "belly" of nylon netting inside the bucket. The netting holes should be 1/4 to 1/2 inches (6 to 12 mm) — small enough that the D/CW does not easily fall through.
- The "belly" should not touch the bottom of the bucket as it is filling, so the net should be suspended a little more than halfway into the bucket to start. This can be adjusted if the load begins to hit bottom but there is still room at the top for deposits.
- Flap the perimeter of the netting over the sides and bind it securely at the outside of the bucket using a bungee cord or other tie. The net should be tied low enough that a screen and lid can still be affixed at the top.
- Cut a piece of window screen to fit over the top of the bucket and secure it so that it can be easily

lifted to deposit C/DW and sawdust. You will use the screen as cover in dry weather or if you have the bucket under a roof covering. If the bucket is exposed outdoors, cover it with a lid if it rains. Throw a tarp or other covering over the lid. You do not want wet moldering C/DW in a bucket!

Keep a bucket of dry sawdust from non-pressure-treated/non-composite wood handy. Each time you add a D/CW deposit to the net inside the bucket, top it off liberally with sawdust. The sawdust will serve as a carbon source, a sponge to absorb leachate and a biofilter to trap odors. When one bucket is full, cover it securely, allow air to circulate through the side hole and let it sit for a full year. It might take longer to finish if the weather is cold or damp.

When the material looks like crumbly, compost-y soil and has a good musky fragrance, it is ready. Use a compost crank or other probing tool to make sure that the material toward the bottom looks consistent with the top layer. You will have at least one active bucket and one or more aging buckets.

If you have enough outdoor space and years to burn before using the C/DW residual, simply set aside an isolated moldering cove. It should be well away from groundwater drainage: a cinderblock enclosure with dirt floor and tarp or other waterproof covering will do nicely. Throw in a handful of dry sawdust to cover new deposits fully. Stop adding to the pile and let it sit for a year before checking to see if it is ready to use as soil enrichment for ornamental plants.

Vermiculture (cultivating worm poop)

Start up: moderate

Learning curve: moderate to demanding

Maintenance: demanding (unattended worms DIE)

Needs: Carbon "brown" waste source; worms; waterproof containers and drainage trays OR dedicated outdoor area; end use for finished soil enhancements; digging tools

Helpful: compost harvesting screen; empathy for wigglers; open-minded, cooperative housemates

Advantages: odorless and fast if done correctly; ideal for apartments and other small dwellings; highly scalable to space and amount of waste; works indoors or out; delights children

Disadvantages: temperature sensitive; harvesting castings requires patience; oh, come on — we're talking about live worms ... possibly under your sink ... under your bed

End products: good eco vibes; incredibly fertile worm castings and worm tea for ornamentals; castings with low salinity (lower than D/CW compost)

There is no better way to channel your inner third grader than wrangling worms! Worm ranchers have hundreds of pets who do nothing but turn unwanted organic material into fertilizer. But like all pets, worms come with a set of responsibilities.

On a household level, most people use worms to cycle food scraps into worm poop, called "castings," a high-value fertilizer. A well-run worm bin will succeed in almost any contained area with good drainage. Worms can thrive in commercial tray systems or small plastic storage bins that fit under the sink. They are happy outdoors if you keep their homes protected and temperate.

Commercial worm breeders often feed their worms manure diets. So, yes, they will "eat" D/CW. I use quotes around "eat" for good reason. Since worms have no teeth or stomachs, they actually ingest nearby bacteria, fungi and protozoa — microorganisms that predigest available food. But to keep it simple, I will use the word "eat" to describe worm consumption.

Worms will eat anything that once lived, including your old cotton sock and my straw hat. First microorganisms attack the organic material and then worms ingest the microorganisms. So food needs to rot or compost a bit to get a worm's attention.

As with any meal, presentation is everything. Things go better if you cut food into smaller pieces to accelerate decomposition. Keep the food moist, mix it with irresistible bits and spice it up with some soil biology. Got that? Now forget about the "irresistible bits" if D/CW is on the menu.

Worms will reliably subsist on a manure diet only if there is nothing better in their world to sustain them. Give them D/CW with a carbon source such as shredded paper, cardboard or sawdust and they will make do, like Scarlett O'Hara in that turnip field at post-war Tara. Another reason for this dietary restriction is that the bacteria already living in D/CW breed quickly in the presence of food scraps. The worms can't keep up with ingesting the bacteria and could die as a result of the concentration.

So please — no desserts, no between-meal snacks, just D/CW and nice damp shredded paper products. Three more simple rules:

- Do not feed worms waste generated by dogs or cats on deworming medication, a sure way to bump off the whole colony.
- Do not use clay cat litter if you plan to use CW as food because it can harm the worms. Do not add

quantities of used corn, wheat, paper or wood litter to the bin. Simply add CW to the paper. Composting is a good way to upcycle this organic litter separately.

Preparing to wrangle worms

If you are ready to give it a go, visit the many excellent websites dedicated to building bins, maintaining colonies and harvesting castings, including the art of D/CW vermiculture. You will even find commercial nesting wormery trays specifically designed for pet waste. These look nice and might prove practical. But there is no need to get into technicalities or complicated systems.

Worms simply need darkness, air, reasonable temperatures, bedding, food and water. Build them a home, tend to their simple needs and make sure they are hearty and multiplying. Do a little online troubleshooting if you run into problems. Here is one quick set of instructions for the beginner.

Step 1: Purchase a pound of red wigglers (Eisenia fetida), available online. These worms do not burrow, thrive in crowded bins and will eat food scraps or D/CW. At around $25–35 a pound, this will be your only real investment. Your pound of worms will live comfortably in two square foot of surface bin area. They will double their population in three months, but will stop reproducing when the population reaches its limit based on space and food.

Red wigglers eat half to all of their weight in food every twenty-four hours. So one pound of worms — approximately a thousand — will eat from half to one pound of food per day. As the population grows to fill your container, their consumption will increase. You can even start new bins using worms from the homestead container.

Since the average dog produces three-quarters of a pound of waste per day, around 1,500 happy worms should do the trick. A larger dog or multiple dogs will require more hungry worms. One thousand worms should serve the purpose for multiple cats. You will need to start slowly and play it by ear so as not to over- or underfeed.

Step 2: Before the arrival of your worms, work on your bin. Worms do not need fancy digs. Two dark plastic storage containers that stack into one another and a single lid will provide a happy home.

- Use two eight- to ten-gallon containers that will fit, when stacked, into the storage area you have in mind — in a cabinet, under the stairs, in a corner of the garage. You will need a fitted lid only for the top bin.
- Drill two sets of holes on the upper container. The first set will be on the sides along the top so that they

are exposed under the lid. These are your air holes.
Then drill several holes around the bottom so that the
leachate or excess water can drain into the container
below.

- Fit the second container under the first to collect
  leachate. You might want to put some bricks or other
  material in the bottom container to lift the top bin
  slightly. This will circulate air and make sure the tea
  cannot rise into the top bin.

Step 3: Bring in the Welcome Wagon! Tear up newspaper and/or cardboard or collect shredded paper and
deposit into the top container. This will provide carbon
and help circulate air and hold moisture. Either dampen
the material and wring it out, or sprinkle/mist it. It should
be damp as a moist sponge, but not dripping.

Step 4: Add the wigglers along with the soil in-
cluded in the shipping box. You might also add a bit
of soil from your yard or potted plants along with just
a bit of D/CW. Cover everything with some shredded
paper and sprinkle with water. A topping of carbon material will keep your new pets moist, hold in any mild
odors and keep out insects.

Step 5: Leave them alone so that they can get ori-
ented, punch their little timecards and settle into work.
Add D/CW slowly until you have an idea of how much

they will eat as they get acquainted with their diet and surroundings. Worms do not like to be disturbed, so keep some of your D/CW in non-pressure-treated/non-composite sawdust and feed it every few days.

Feed as food disappears. If you see that too much is accumulating, slack off. Some experts suggest tossing in a small sprinkling of bokashi mix every three to four weeks to spice up the microbial menu.

Keep the bin somewhere no colder than 40°F (4°C) or hotter than 80°F (26°C). Do not place it near vibrating appliances or equipment. If your bin is outdoors, make sure the lid is always secure so that the worms do not dry out or drown. Earthworms need a thin layer of water around them that enables them to breathe through their skin. The material around them needs to feel damp and crumbly. Wetter is better ... that is why the bins are constructed to drain off excess moisture.

Worms try to escape only if the bin is so wet that they have problems breathing through their skin. The container should not be smelly unless the beds become anaerobic from too much food or moisture. Mixing a little calcium carbonate with the bedding can alleviate this problem. Small flies will appear only if there is not enough bedding or you do not cover the food with moist shredded paper.

If you have space, you can start a D/CW worm farm outdoors and nurture a stable wiggler colony that will successfully overwinter. Deep piles of soil retain heat and allow worms to migrate lower to survive through cold months. Grass clippings, leaves and D/CW will keep a pound of red wigglers fat and happy. You can surround your worm home with hay bales or fencing, but avoid cedar, redwood and pine.

If there are moles in your area, install screens at the bottom to keep your worm beds from becoming a free buffet. Covering beds with carpeting will keep in moisture and provide shade in the summer protection in the winter. Bury a cache of D/CW in the center/bottom of the pile before a deep freeze.

You've got to love my friend Liz. Her extensive outdoor ranch feasts on every bit of "edible" household garbage. Every fall she fills the family's spent jack-o-lanterns with worm treats and buries them in her well-protected wiggler bins. She hasn't lost a colony yet.

Industrial containers, tubs and tanks are perfect outdoor wormeries if the bottoms are drilled to facilitate drainage. Discarded refrigerators with added drainage are also reliable worm containers. You can even run a D/CW worm farm in the freezer compartment while feeding worms food scraps in the refrigerator section. Many websites provide instructions for customizing old appliances for this purpose.

When D/CW has disappeared and castings (grainy, rich soil) have accumulated, you can harvest the vermicompost. Kids love to help! Spread the container contents out on a tarp or trash bag. Do this in moderate sunlight or under a bright indoor light. The light will make the worms burrow under the surface.

Give them time to escape and then rake the top layer of castings. Wait for the next batch of worms to retreat deeper and rake off another layer until the worms literally have nowhere to hide. Return the worms and remaining castings to a fresh bed of damp paper. Tiny worms and eggs that were raked up with the vermicompost will benefit your garden.

You can also harvest castings using a sifter, which can be as simple to build as nailing quarter- or eighth-inch screening to a frame of two-by-fours. The sifter can be small or large to suit your needs. People with outdoor piles or bins can simply lure worms to specific areas with food or by shoveling vermicompost from sections where worms are not feeding.

The big payoff of worm wrangling is "black gold!" Worm castings or vermicompost is much richer in plant-available nutrients and biological compounds like

plant-growth hormones than regular compost. Gardeners pay a premium price for bagged castings. Worm mucus in the vermicompost also captures soil nutrients often washed away during watering.

A word of caution about the liquid that runs off the bottom. This is called "leachate," NOT "tea." It can be diluted and used on plants with caution, but it might contain pathogens and compounds harmful to plants. Worms need a moist environment, but too much liquid will fill all the pore space and eliminate air, which they also need. This is why drainage is important for all vermicompost systems.

A few words about dung beetles

Paleontologists have found dung balls rolled by scarab beetles and fossilized thirty million years ago. The thousands of dung beetle species have had excrement on their menu for a long time and are set in their ways. Some transport dung, some tunnel under it and some "dwellers" are simply dung couch potatoes. All of them keep the earth's surface clear of animal waste, sometimes eliminating whole piles within hours. They also diminish methane released into the air, and enrich and aerate the soil.

You might have seen online chat about using dung beetles to clean up areas frequented by dogs. In fact, dung beetles can be purchased online for that purpose, and success stories occasionally circulate on doggie blogs. Ranchers routinely release them to control livestock patties in pastures, so why not put them to use in yards and dog parks?

A liquid extract can be made from finished vermicompost. This is what is often referred to as "tea." There is abundant information posted on the Internet about this very useful liquid. One of the best free, reliable online publication on the subject is "Tea Time in the Tropics," authored by scientists at the University of Hawaii.

Commercially produced and tested worm-poo products may be certified safe for agriculture. But do not use DIY vermicompost or tea from worms that dined on D/CW for edible vegetables and fruits.

Yes, there it is — that dire warning again: however you upcycle the stuff, however careful you are, keep

You might think that because these insects eat dung, they're not fussy. But some species have their own dietary preferences. The beetles you release might resist your dog's waste and jump ship for the rabbit hutch next door. You can't corral a flying insect. And there are other factors that make this a dubious choice:

- pesticides and flea/ticks/worming treatments will kill beetles,

- dung beetles often eat only animal waste from their place of origin, and

- during extremely cold or dry weather, dung beetles hibernate.

That said, dung beetles are eco-friendly insects in decline. So if you're feeling adventurous, find the right species and provide an attractive environment with plenty of fresh DW, there's no harm in experimenting.

processed D/CW away from edibles. Several studies have shown that vermicomposting can kill pathogens. The Orange County (Florida) Environmental Protection Division (OCEPD) carried out an experiment using earthworms to process contaminated biosolids into Class A soil amendment. The agency succeeded in stabilizing the full range of pathogen indicators, including fecal

coliform, salmonella, enteric virus and helminth ova.
[31] But even if worms magically sanitize 100 percent of everything passing through their guts, there is no DIY system that can keep undigested and contaminated bits of D/CW waste out of the harvested castings and tea. So play it safe and do not use untested pet-soil products on from food crops.

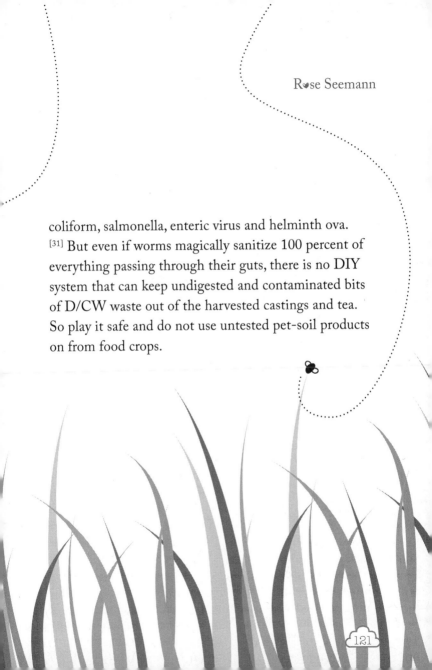

Chapter Four

Mission possible: "gold star" DW compost

Down the rabbit hole

Yfou've read about the many ways you can remove pet waste from that slippery downhill slope to the landfill. When you upcycle household D/CW, your dog or cat will be just a whisker away from net zero carbon paw prints! But is it possible to upcycle tons of pet waste and produce a safe, productive fertilizer? How hard would that be? And what properties would the resulting material have? I found the answers to those questions and started EnviroWagg, a company that converts DW into a resource.

Every Monday our neighborhood curbs are studded with recycling bins full of paper, glass, plastic and gleaming aluminum cans. Some cities also tackle the messier and more labor-intensive services of yard and food waste composting. Most people are happy to sort and separate recyclable items if professionals take it from there. And they're even happier if the service creates jobs and generates revenue or saves money. Municipalities have ground yard waste into mulch for generations, and more and more communities are recycling food scraps. Considering the enormous amount of D/CW trashed each year, shouldn't we be working just as hard to find a way to upcycle that waste, too?

And so, when considering my options, I asked myself, "What would it take to initiate an upcycling program in the United States that would include D/CW?" I came up with these possibilities:

- Develop omni-organics-to-power systems such as biodigestion and gasification (expensive, few existing models).
- Use the existing flush systems and treat the material as a sewage biosolid (would overwhelm current treatment facilities and increase water usage).
- Systematically scrub the pathogens during processing so that safe residuals can be distributed as a soil amendment (no one is doing this).

Was it even possible to kill the bad bugs in pet waste during an upcycling process? Could D/CW produce soil amendments safe for vegetable gardens? Did pet waste offer a special oomph to green up plants? Surely I wasn't the only person curious about the possibilities of reducing pollution while converting four percent of scorned residential trash into something useful. Right out of the gate, I found two documented dog-waste composting projects, one conducted in the United States and the other in Canada.

"Dog Waste Composting Study," the USDA Natural Resources Conservation Service in Fairbanks, Alaska, gave

sled dog yard managers the green light on composting dog waste to reduce pollution of local waterways. The report offered step-by-step instructions and suggested that the resulting compost be used to enrich soil around ornamental plants.

Researchers at Concordia University in Montreal, Quebec, conducted a 2007 study, "Design, Testing and Implementation of a Large-Scale Urban Dog Waste Composting Program," detailing a successful volunteer program at Notre Dame de Grace Dog Park in Montreal. Both of these projects demonstrated the viability of DW composting. When carefully processed, the material emitted no odor and produced rich finished compost.

I found that several parks had officially investigated possibilities or tried dead-end experiments with DW composting. Denali National Park in Alaska was a stand-out success. Volunteers there had been composting dog-waste since 1980, using the material for ornamental park plantings and making it available to nearby residents. But I could find no enterprise processing D/CW compost that tested consistently safe for commercial distribution, which would be the key to financial sustainability.

Around the same time, Paul, an acquaintance in Chicago who owned a pooper-scooper service, e-mailed some intriguing photos. He was dismayed by the quantity of DW his business was pitching into dumpsters and wondered if it had any use whatsoever. Would it work as a fertilizer?

Paul installed two raised beds near his house and planted tomatoes, broccoli and green beans in each. Both beds had the same garden soil, sunlight and watering schedule. He sprinkled one, per instructions, with a popular water-soluble, chemical nitrogen fertilizer. He buried some dry DW in the second bed, never intending to harvest the DW-fed veggies as a food crop.

Let me say that I trust this guy. He is honest. He was not trying to prove anything of commercial value. He had nothing to gain. He was simply tired of filling dumpsters with DW and wanted to see if it would help to make something grow.

Paul's photos of the mature plants could knock off a cat's socks. The vegetables fertilized with DW were huge — useless but huge — compared to their rivals. Evaluations show that DW has a 40 percent higher nitrogen content than cow manure.[11] Who knows? If this stuff were properly processed and de-bugged for public use, gardeners might come up with some horticultural delights. But no one had tested pathogen-safe D/CW compost for plant nutrients.

I had to chase this rabbit down the hole. My first task was finding out if DW is a viable source material for

compost that is safe for distribution. I needed, as they say, professional help. So I called every composting professional in a 50-mile radius of Metro Denver to propose a project involving DW. A few rude ones laughed outright and many nice ones tried to talk me down. The ones somewhere in between honestly did not know what to say except "no" and "good luck."

When I ran out of the "compost" listings, I moved on to farmers, hoping that one of them might share my curiosity and give it a try. After much disbelief and many rejections, one of my contacts gave me a lead! He referred me to a farmer's son who was "just the kind of fella who might want to try something like that."

Was he handing me off to a full-blown eccentric? Would this meet-up involve a pickup truck plastered with dubious bumper stickers and dangling with dream catchers?

My first phone conversation with Brian put my concerns to rest. He heard me out and invited me to his home turf so that we could discuss the project. I drove north from Denver along a main highway past strip malls, scrap yards and open prairie. On this warm May afternoon, the air wafted the dusky aroma of newly applied fertilizer.

A winding exit and an arrow-straight county road took me to my destination. I waited under a cottonwood tree on the edge of a field within earshot of lowing cows.

Stately ridges of loose earth ran north–south toward a vanishing point, mirroring the Front Range just to the west. I would soon learn to identify these ridges as compost windrows, tall as storefronts and churned by huge mechanized turners that straddle the rows.

As it turned out, the farmer who sent me his way was right. Brian was a smart, affable guy who had been composting cow manure since he was 15. Now 29, he had a thriving mulch, compost and soil business. Brian enjoyed talking about fine-tuning processes, redesigning equipment, experimenting with crops. His enthusiasm was infectious.

I laid out my idea about trying to compost dog-waste. He listened intently and stared off at nothing in particular. What on earth was he thinking?

When there was no more left to say, I asked him what he thought: "Are you game?" After a long pause, he asked me to deliver the DW. He mulled over the situation a bit and added, "Three tons to start." We shook hands on it.

Alrighty then. All I needed was three tons of DW. Or, as Donald Duck's inventor buddy Gyro Gearloose would say, "Three tons of dog-waste … how to get it?"

I took a spin to a regional Humane Society adoption center not far from the composting site. I explained "our" (no longer "my!") project to the director, who was amused

and more than helpful. He asked the staff to designate "dog poop only" bins, which they were more than happy to fill with big garbage bags bulging with DW.

On Fridays I rented a pickup truck, emptied the bins into the bed, and hauled out a fresh load of bagged DW. I'm a bit embarrassed to say that now and then, craving some company, I roped my husband in on these excursions. "Why don't you start an online chocolate business like your friend Karen?" he would ask. But love conquers all.

One hot summer afternoon, I was grateful to have an accomplice at the wheel. Chuck and I were transporting a load of DW along a stretch of I-25 when an accident ahead brought traffic to a standstill. When this sort of thing happens, drivers get out of their cars, hoist themselves up for a look-see, saunter around and gather in clumps to discuss the situation. Police appear.

The sun was cooking the bagged DW. Even in the truck cab, I could feel the odor spreading and seeping onto my clothes, my hair, my skin. There is absolutely no noxious smell quite like lots and lots of warm, raw DW. One by one the milling motorists were getting wind of the state of affairs — no comments yet but heads turning, sniffing around for the source.

Chuck took quick evasive action. He pulled that pickup right off the road, across a ditch, over a grassy hillside and onto a service road. How he did it without losing the load defied the laws of physics.

Several months passed before Brian sized things up and said, "Enough." I swear we had way more than three tons, but who was I to quibble. In any case, it was hard to tell. Friday after Friday I would pull up to the farm with my weekly load. That stuff was as heavy as wet concrete and the bags were as ungainly as a pregnant sow belly. But I managed to drag the loads across the truck bed and hurl them over the side into the waiting bucket of Brian's front loader.

We did not have enough material to generate a windrow. But Brian thought we had just enough to process several static piles by turning the DW, bulking agents and natural stimulants with the front loader. He monitored temperatures and tried several recipes to get the best results. With Brian the question was never, "Can I get it to compost?" but "Can I turn this DW into an exceptional soil amendment?"

Dealing with small plastic pickup bags was a dilemma we would cope with later when servicing dog parks. The shelter that supplied our first raw material used scoopers for cleanup, so these first loads consisted of loose DW in standard trash bags that were easy to slice open and eliminate. So the process could begin quickly.

Of course, my composting partner was no longer dealing with your run-of-the-mill dairy-cow manure. This was carnivore waste from shelter dogs, which was likely to contain a whole slew of stubborn pathogens, including the dreaded helminth ova. These microscopic roundworm eggs are as tough to kill as blockbuster movie aliens. The EPA considers them to be "indicators" — once you've eliminated these babies, other parasites that might inflict mayhem are toast.

To ensure that biosolid products distributed for public use are safe, the EPA provides time-temperature regimes for processing. An overheated, sterile soil amendment would offer no value for plants. But compost for commercial distribution must have a pathogen mix that is severely damaged or destroyed.

Thermal treatment requirements start at 122°F (50°C). In order to meet EPA requirements, samples of finished material must be tested and found to contain no viable helminth ova and demonstrate specific low density levels for either fecal coliforms or Salmonella bacteria. [14]

But simply following regulations for nuking pathogens will not necessarily produce heavenly compost. Heat the compost up too long or at too high a temperature and you might kill the good biology. The EPA keeps us safe but has no interest in delighting us with the resulting products.

Consumer Product Safety Commission regulations ensure that your PJs won't spontaneously combust, but that's no guarantee that they will be warm and snuggly yet alluring to your significant other.

Backyard composting can be a lark. Professional composting is an art as well as a serious science. This is particularly the case when working with nontraditional materials potentially containing stubborn pathogens. The heat generated by thermophilic action is only one of the destructive forces. During heat-up and cool-down, a diverse population of mesophilic organisms competes for food within the compost pile. In the process, they consume pathogens and produce antibiotics. Throughout the cooling phase and long curing (resting) period, earthworms, protozoa, fungi and insects further continue dismantling the original material.

So a master composter is a bit like a symphony conductor. The maestro makes sure that each orchestral section has an excellent mix of strong microbial players and then directs them with competence, perfect timing and grace. This is not an exaggeration. After several years of observation, I can confidently say that serious composting is a blend of technique, experience and instinct undertaken by a darned good scientist.

While composting can be as lazy or as exacting as you want it to be, Brian was not a complacent guy. It didn't

take me long to realize I had stumbled onto a rare individual. Not only was he truly excited about the prospect of natural soil enrichment, he also had a streak of genius with machinery and a knack for promotion. Here was a guy who had bargained with industry soil buyers since he was a teenager. He was determined to make the best DW compost known to humankind.

Brian experimented with composting the material as a "biosolid" or "sludge" per EPA instructions, [16] a real page-turner document. These are the same guidelines applied to processing sewage before it is approved for distribution or agricultural applications. In other words, the same guidelines used to treat the stuff you flush down the toilet before the residue is OK for fertilizing your grocery store produce.

The resulting DW compost was homogenous in texture and color, dark brown and fluffy. Best of all, the material had the wonderful fragrance of fresh, rich springtime soil. Oooo, lovely! But was all that lively biology good biology? Was the compost safe for people and plants?

The Environmental Quality Laboratory at Colorado State University tested a sample. The DW compost passed on the first try! The material was officially free of EPA-indicator pathogens and safe to use on edible plants. But did the compost contain anything harmful to plants? Would the lovely fluffy stuff provide a hearty square meal for plants? Was there anything extraordinary about it?

Colorado Analytical Laboratories evaluated samples to determine basic plant nutrients. Results showed that the compost offered an impressive balance of nitrogen, phosphorus and potassium — building blocks for healthy plants. The pH (acidity/alkalinity ratio) was in the neutral range. Salinity was similar to levels in other manure-based compost.

So far, so good. On paper, at least, it looked like our DW compost would support greenery and do no harm. But there are so many micro-nutrients and living organisms that add up to a rich compost blend. We would need to do some comparative tests on actual plants.

Plant power unleashed!

And so we moved on to the next key phase of our project: the part where sensitive plant roots meet Rover's treasure. The composting project had come full circle by the following spring, so the timing was right for planting trials. I contacted universities, consultants and nurseries, but could find no feasible third parties to conduct a plant test. My contacts were long on credibility, but either had no interest in the project (oh, ick!) or required funding much too substantial for our modest experiment. So I

decided that, as a garden hobbyist, I would conduct some-
what informal tests on my own.

How would the DW compost perform as a growing
medium for fledgling houseplants? I decided to try it on
variegated spider plants because they are hardy, root and
grow quickly and tolerate screened sunlight. I removed
two dozen plantlets from shoots and rooted them in water.
Then I chose the twelve transplants most similar in size
and root development to use in the experiment.

My goal was to compare DW compost to "Premium"
poultry waste-based (PPW) compost that I purchased at a
local garden center. (Chicken waste is the richest barnyard
manure with high nitrogen content.) I also wanted to see
how the transplants responded to various concentrations
of both composts to make sure that high doses of DW
compost (30 percent) would not stress new roots.

I prepared four soil mixtures.

#1 - 15% DW compost,
85% peat moss

#2 - 30% DW compost,
70% peat moss

#3 - 15% PPW compost,
85% peat moss

#4 - 30% PPW compost,
70% peat moss

I started with twelve identical pressure-formed plastic
nursery pots. I filled each pot with 2.2 liters of soil:

three pots with mixture #1
three pots with mixture #2

three pots with mixture #3
three pots with mixture #4.

T hen I planted the twelve baby spiders, placed the transplant pots in shallow plastic nursery trays and set them under a shade fabric in an open, sunny corner of our deck. I gave them each half a cup of water every third day, and rotated the trays and turned the pots every third day to provide uniform light exposure.

After two-and-a-half weeks, the leaves on the transplants in the DW compost mixture were nearly twice as long as the leaves of the plants in the PPW mixture. Both the DW and PPW plants in the 30-percent compost mixes were visibly heartier than both sets of plants in the 15-percent compost mixes. The 30-percent compost DW plants had twice the amount of foliage as the 30-percent PPW plants. So a relatively high concentration of DW compost did not compromise the plantlets.

This growth trend continued. As the plants grew, I increased the water input but kept the amount and schedule consistent among all of the plants. While there were quasiruns and overachievers in each of the soil mixtures, ten weeks later the DW spiders were conspicuously more robust than the PPW spiders. You might say they were the tarantulas of the plant trays. The DW plants began sending out long arms of plantlet shoots right and left.

I asked visitors which plants looked heartier and no one failed to spot the doggie plants. They screamed

"alpha." If we had set up a ten-round match pitting any DW plant versus any PPW plant, PPW would have kissed the canvas.

I also wanted to know if seeds would safely germinate and take root using the DW compost. So I bought a packet of "choice mixture" petunia seeds, two identical flats of 48 plastic planting cups with drainage holes and two sets of plastic bottom trays with transparent hoods. I prepared two simple batches of planting mixtures:

- 50% DW compost and 50% perlite
- 50% PPW compost and 50% perlite

I filled each of 48 pots in Tray 1 with three rounded tablespoons of the DW mixture and each of 48 cups in Tray 2 with three rounded tablespoons of the PPW mixture. I saturated the soils in both trays and topped off the mixture in each cup with one rounded tablespoon of slightly crushed perlite. I arranged three tiny petunia seeds on the perlite in each cup, then generously sprayed both seeded flats and covered them with the plastic hood.

I placed the trays on an ironing board in a window where they would each receive several hours of direct morning sunlight. I switched the trays daily to ensure that they received an equal amount of light. I irrigated from the bottom trays with the same amounts of water. I misted both trays equally when either of the tops appeared dry. I snipped the smallest shoots to yield one plant per cup.

All of the petunias began sprouting at roughly the same time. But in 40 days, the petunias in the DW mixture had visibly surpassed the PPW petunias. The oval leaves were much larger and more numerous.

A week later, the difference was even more dramatic. So it would seem that when the roots of the sprouts began drawing on the nutrients below the perlite, the DW compost mixture jump-started the petunias. The petunias feasting on DW began blooming first — whites, purples, clown-faced mottles. And pink ... every conceivable shade of pink.

So our first batch of DW compost tested negative for EPA-indicator pathogens, positive for plant nutrients, and had, in fact, produced very impressive results in informal but rigorous and documented trials ... on my deck ... on my ironing board. It was time to get our product into circulation.

For the most part, hobby gardening is seasonal. During three months of excitement, customers plan, work the soil, select materials and install major plantings. That enthusiasm levels off into a mellow period when a gardener simply sizes up, maintains and enjoys the results.

Mid-March to mid-June is the narrow window when most gardeners improve their soil. That first spring I had test results and hands-on proof that the doggie compost was, indeed, "gold star." Now I needed some creds — gardeners to back up or disprove my experiences.

The seasonal window was closing quickly. I had just a few weeks to get feedback. Brian and I bagged up the finished compost in 0.5 cubic foot quantities. I took bags of DW compost to all the open-minded gardeners I knew who were installing flower beds, transplanting trees and planting in containers. The bags featured instructions on mixing the compost with existing soil to improve nutrient content, microbial activity, porosity and water retention.

I gave the doggie compost to the owner of a feed supply store that planted hundreds of annuals in boxes surrounding the parking lot. I supplied compost to a scooper service with a potted tropical plant sunning in an office window. A neighbor tried the DW compost on a single cotoneaster bush in a hedgerow.

It took quite a while for the stories to filter back, but the comments were gratifying. "Flowers are the best ever!" "Humongous new leaves!" "Look at that bright green!"

My next job was getting the word out on the cheap and gathering stories about how the compost performed. I set up a vendor table at pet and gardening events, handing out free small sample bags of compost to "green up houseplants." I asked visitors to e-mail their observations. One indoor gardener tried it on one of her orchid cuttings. Only the doggie soil produced a bloom. She sent photos. Another fed the DW compost to an exhausted philodendron that rebounded. Another used it to grow grass in turf that the dog had destroyed — sweet irony! The stories multiplied — anecdotal, but exciting to hear!

This was good news for my partner, who continued to experiment with recipes and methods. How was the C/N ratio? Were the inoculants doing the job? His goal was now "platinum star."

There is no shortage of raw material for our project. Since we began composting, parks, dog day cares, animal shelters, veterinarians — even a dog-friendly bar — have contracted for our composting services. Pet Scoop, the area's largest dog-waste remediation service, now transports much of the DW, saving fuel necessary for duplicate collection routes and giving eco-savvy owner Sam one more opportunity to practice sustainability. Our hauler, Terry, uses a 20-foot, 7,500-pound capacity trailer to haul 8-feet-long, 800-pound bags of DW from two dog parks with in-ground container systems. We encourage clients to use scoopers and compostable bags, but as long as plastic pickup bags are Standard Operating

Procedure for Dog People, plastic will continue to work
its way into our composting system. We shred all material at the start to expose as much DW as possible to
heat and air. Certified compostable bags degrade totally,
but we need to screen out pieces of "biodegradable" and
regular plastic bags. These pieces are trashed at the end
of this step in the process.

We proudly service the first zero-waste dog park in
Boulder, Colorado, and are embarking on a pilot program
to upcycle DW from three of its many trailheads. Boulder
provides certified compostable bags and separate trash
and DW collection bins. In addition to mitigating the
environmental impact of trashed DW, the city hopes to

encourage pickup along its system of breathtaking foot-
hills trails. But because certified compostable bags cost
more than twice as much as ordinary plastic bags, many
other cities believe they are too expensive for park budgets.
To further lower costs, they often encourage Dog People
to bring their own bags and stuff extra plastic ones into
PVC tubes stationed along walkways.

If parks services are willing to provide standard-sized
pickup bags and designate separate bins for DW, we are
willing to take the extra step needed to eliminate plastic.
If the plastic becomes a problem with large-scale production, we might need to refuse to accept them at the source.
Eventually plastic bag bans will increase the demand for

compostable bags and drive down prices. When that happens, petro-based products — so last century! — will no longer complicate our lives in so many ways.

DW compost was getting two green thumbs up from friends and total strangers. And test marketing had resulted in modest sales of bagged DW compost at local garden centers. Ramping up production will be easy using a large compost tumbler. But will people buy it in the quantities needed to turn a profit?

Yes, we have come to the heart of the matter: Will high-quality, plant-empowering DW compost products sell? Will the biological symmetry resonate with consumers? Will the elegance of upcycling and the promise of smaller carbon paw prints override the tiresome "ick" factor? Even a socially conscious endeavor needs to be financially sustainable. We will need to sell this lovely compost in order to keep producing it. Informed consumers are always key to closing the recycling loop. But fiscal viability is our next adventure: another story for another time.

Chapter Five

Conclusion

We are collecting and composting just a tiny fraction of the DW generated in the Denver metro area. But the amount we remove and process is enough to literally and figuratively take your breath away. Two of the busy off-leash parks we service generate 2,400 pounds (1.1 tonnes) of DW each month. And that is less than 0.01 percent of this single community's doggie output. Do we get discouraged? No! We're like that beetle merrily rolling his dung ball, not Sisyphus pushing his boulder, devoid of hope.

For starters, I've just had a chance to tell you the facts about the mountains of D/CW challenging our cities,

trash collections and sanitary landfills. And you now know that you can choose to be 100-percent successful approaching zero waste with your own pets. That's gratifying! Once you Know Better, it will be hard to leave Fido's gift where it lies. You might even feel a niggling annoyance when you trash your pet waste. Hooray!

When Know Better opens the door just a tad, Do Something shoves in his big gangly foot and you're Stuck With It! Maybe you'll consider the best way to reduce your D/CW landfill stream and give it your best shot. And maybe you'll encourage local officials to find

solutions to mitigate dog waste pollution at parks, trails or bike paths via upcycling; these solutions can include strategies as easy as burying waste in a trench topped off with a new landscaping feature or building a simple high-capacity septic system. Or you can join in an effort to secure a biodigester or compost facility that accepts all organic waste.

Suppose you can't reach a recycling goal dear to your heart without help. Those nearest to you — friends, family, significant other — might not be as motivated as you, or even vaguely interested. Don't let that take the caffeine out of your brew. Find people who want to make the same changes as you or might have something to gain by getting involved. Keep moving forward. When you Know Better and then Do Something, your perspective shifts radically. Like that dung beetle doing its damnedest, the vastness of what you cannot do no longer overwhelms you. A whole herd of cows is mucking up the pasture, but it doesn't faze that beetle. The dung ball he's rolling and then burying will help make the world a better place.

What does it take to be a pet steward truly into sustainability? If you search online for "green pet supplies," you'll find hundreds of products, including

- all-natural treats in pouches impossible to recycle,
- hypoallergenic cat wipes to be trashed after one use,
- tiny plastic dispensers filled with "biobags guaranteed to degrade in landfills,"
- "eco-friendly" nylon breakaway cat collars,
- "non-toxic" dayglow poly-based toys.

urable, fun purchases are better choices than cheap, dangerous products. But consider this: vendors using "green" branding are saying you instinctively Know Better (believe their environmental pitch) and should Do Something (move your cursor to the shopping cart). The fact that these supplies even exist means that resources were excavated or harvested, products were manufactured and shipped — sometimes around the world — from factory to distribution center. All of these activities are fossil intensive! There's nothing wrong with indulging in judicious consumption. Commerce keeps us all in kibble. But let's not kid ourselves into thinking we're environmentalists because we buy "green" pet supplies.

If you want to reduce your pet's carbon paw print:

- create pet toys out of safe, leftover items, fabrics or yarn.
- buy local natural pet foods, prepare fresh food or serve leftover human food that will not harm pets.
- take your dog to a garden to nibble on his favorite fresh veggies.

- nick nack patty whack, give a dog a ham bone.
- choose collars, leashes and toys that are made locally from recyclable or recycled materials.

And, of course, seriously consider upcycling your household pet waste. The average dog generates 275 pounds (125 kg) of waste every year. Chances are good that's more than you weigh! Imagine diverting that body bag alone from your trash. If enough Dog and Cat People send their pet's waste back to nature, we can lighten our collective environmental impact in a significant way. And this gift to Mother Earth will trump all the eco-friendly nibbles and knickknacks your dollars can buy.

Are you game?

"Only when we see that we are part of the totality of the planet, not a superior part with special privileges, can we work effectively to bring about an earth restored to wholeness." — Elizabeth Watson, Quaker

Notes:

1. US Environmental Protection Agency, Landfill Methane and Outreach Programs, 2013.

2. US Environmental Protection Agency, *Federal Register*, v. 53, no. 168, August 30, 1988, p. 33.

3. "Portland Company Will Compost Your Dog Waste," Jacques Van Lunen, *The Oregonian*, Oregon Live, February 2, 2010.

4. "Who Knew? Upcycling the Dog Poo" (composting dog waste from Allan H. Treman Marine State Park, Ithaca, N.Y.), Joanna M. Foster, Green — A Blog About Energy and the Environment, *The New York Times*, April 2, 2012.

5. "Here's the Scoop: San Francisco to Turn Dog Poop Into Biofuel," *National Geographic New*s, October 28, 2010.

6. "2006 Parks Waste Audit — Final Report", City of Toronto Parks, Forestry and Recreation, Parks Standards and Innovation, December 2006.

7. "Analysis of 2006 Colorado Waste Stream — Initial Findings", Colorado Department of Public Health and Environment Pollution Prevention Advisory Board, January 22, 2008.

8. California Fish and Game Code, 4501.

9. Dealing with Dog Waste in Vancouver Parks / Preliminary Research for Dog Waste Composting at Everett Crowley Park, LEES + Associates Landscape Architects.

10. US Environmental Protection Agency, National Pollutant Discharge Elimination System (NPDES), Pet Waste Management.

11. "Design, Testing and Implementation of a Large-Scale Urban Dog Waste Composting Program", Concordia University, Montreal, Quebec, Canada, Autumn 2007.

12. Dog Waste Becomes Power Plant for Park, Associated Press, September 22, 2010.

13. *Veterinary Toxicology: Basic and Clinical Principles*, edited by Ramesh C. Gupta, 2007.

14. "Toxoplasma gondii oocyst survival under defined temperatures", Dubey, J., *Journal of Parasitology*, pp. 862–62, 1998.

15. Pet Care, Toxoplasmosis, American Society for the Prevention of Cruelty to Animals (ASPCA), 2014.

16. "Control of Pathogens and Vector Attraction in Sewage Sludge", Environmental Regulations and Technology, US Environmental Protection Agency, Revised July 2003.

17. Poo Power: Zoo Electrified by Elephant-poo, *Animal Planet*, Animals in the News, October 11, 2011.

18. California Legislative Information, SB-567 Recycling: plastic products, (DeSaulnier, 2011–12), October 8, 2011.

19. "Heavy Metals Availability and Fractions in Soil Amended with Biosolid Composts", M.D. Revoredo, A.A.D. Cintra, L.T. Braz, W.J. Melo, ISHS *Acta Horticulturae* 762: XXVII International Horticultural Congress–IHC2006: International Symposium on Horticultural Plants in Urban and Peri-Urban Life.

20. "Remediation of heavy metals from urban waste by vermicomposting using earthworms: Eudrilus eugeniae, Eisenia fetida and Perionyx excavatus", Swati Pattnaik, M. Vikram Reddy, *International Journal of Environment and Waste Management*, 2012 Vol. 10, No. 2/3, pp. 284–96.

21. *Cradle to Cradle, Remaking the Way We Make Things*, William McDonough and Michael Braungart, 2002.

22. "River and Sea Otters and Toxoplasma gondii", The Seadoc Society, Winter 2007.

23. "Parasite in Cats Killing Sea Otters", *NOAA Magazine*, National Oceanic and Atmospheric Administration, January 21, 2003.

24. Urban Agriculture Notes, Pet Waste Composting, *City Farmer*, Canada's Office of Urban Agriculture, Revised September 7, 2012.

the **Pet Poo** pocket guide

25. "Green Bin Program ... From curb to compost", *Living in Toronto*, Toronto, Ontario, no date but live 2014.

26. Powered by poo: Students use dog waste to light park, *ASU News*, Arizona State University, May 1, 2012.

27. "Anaerobic Digestion and Other Alternatives for Dog Waste Management and Education in Thurston County", Aimee Christy, Pacific Shellfish Institute, January 3, 2013.

28. "Comparative Study of the Potential of Dog Waste for Biogas Production", E.C. Okoroigwe, C.N. Ibeto and C.G. Okpara, National Center for Energy and Research Development, University of Nigeria, 2010.

29. Dog Off Leash Area Strategy, 2012–2021, City of Surrey, B.C.

30. "Composting Dog Waste", USDA Natural Resources Conservation Service and the Fairbanks Soil and Water District, 2005.

31. "Achieving Pathogen Stabilization Using Vermicomposting", Bruce R. Eastman, *BioCycle*, November 1999, pp. 62–64.

Acknowledgments

Kathy Doesken reviewed this book to ensure that it accurately explains the complex do-si-do of microbes, protozoa, fungi, earthworms, insects and chemicals involved in organic degradation. Kathy was educated as a soil scientist and pursued her profession in the area of nutrient management at Colorado State University. She lives on a horse farm near Fort Collins, CO, where she crafts high quality vermicompost using organic residues from the farm and community.

Dick Mathes patiently answered my questions regarding the distinctions among recycled, "biodegradable," biodigestable and certified compostable pickup bags. Dick has spent 35 years in various sales and product development positions in the international plastics industry and is currently co-owner of Custom Bioplastics in Burlington, Washington. When Dog People want advice on choosing pickup bags, his first question is always, "What are your disposal options?"

Ann Rippy, Conservation Agronomist, USDA NRCS, was part of the pioneering team that conducted a study on keeping Alaska waterways clean by composting waste at sled dog yards. The project resulted in the United States Department of Agriculture report "Composting Dog Waste." Ann was ever responsive and encouraging: "Yes, it can be done."

Index:

A

American Pet Products Association (APPA), 6

American Recovery and Reinvestment Act (ARRA), 8

American Society for Testing and Materials (ASTM), 48

American Society for the Prevention of
Cruelty to Animals (ASPCA), 44

B

bags
biodegradable, 45, 47
certified compostable, 67, 142–44
hydro-biodegradable, 59

biodigesters, 27, 43, 68, 74, 82, 150

biodigestion, 40, 48, 68–69, 76–77, 93, 125
as anaerobic process, 75
as upcycling, 71

biomass gasification system, 42

biosolids, 39, 91, 120, 132, 134
turned into fertilizer, 62

bokashi, 30, 39, 50, 70, 72, 102, 104
as anaerobic process, 74–76, 78, 82, 84
as recycle method, 40, 49, 79–80

bokashi mixture, 57, 59, 67, 73, 76–77, 79–83, 102–3, 115

Brinton, William, 72

Brown, Jerry, 49

burial, of pet waste, 29, 40, 48, 62–65, 67, 82, 92

C

cat waste
   generation of, 12
   history of, 10
   statistics on, 20
   See also dog waste; pet waste
Chert Glades Master Naturalists (Joplin, MO), 33
Cityfarmer.org, 69, 71
CKWS TV News, 33
clay litters, 10, 12, 19, 22–24, 29, 93, 112
Colorado Analytical Laboratories, 135
compost. See composting; dog waste compost;
   moldering; pet waste compost
composters, 68, 75, 133
   and pet waste, 25
composting, 32–33, 42, 99, 106, 112, 129, 134–35, 141
   as aerobic, 68, 75
   with bokashi, 102, 104
   as destroying pathogens, 38–39
   of food scraps, 25, 124
   high-heat, 30
   as organic recycling, 19, 40
   as process, 48, 82, 84–86, 88–90, 92–97, 133
   for sustainable park maintenance, 77
Consumer Product Safety Commission, 133
Consumer Reports magazine, 51
Cosmo Dog Park (Gilbert, AZ), 77

D

Denali National Park, 126

digesters, 27, 76–77

   See also biodigesters

dog waste

   generation of, 11, 148, 153

   history of, 5

   as issue, 12

   statistics on, 16, 18

   See also cat waste; pet waste

dog waste compost

   for plants, 134, 136, 139–41, 144

   See also composting; moldering

dog waste composting project, 14, 26, 125

dog waste digester, 33, 77

   See also digesters

downcycling, 54

dung beetles, 118–19, 151

E

E-TURD (Energy Transformation
Using Reactive Digestion), 77

E. coli, 57

Environmental Protection Agency (EPA), 36, 139

   and composting, 32

   and flushing, 26, 58

   and landfill liners, 9

   regulations of, 49, 132

   standards of, 39, 56, 91

EnviroWagg, 14, 124
essential microorganisms (EM), 73, 75–76, 102, 104

F

Fairbanks Soil and Water Conservation, 90
FEDOG (Prague), 47
flushing, of pet waste, 26, 29, 40, 48, 57–58, 61

G

Gibson, T., 39
Goldberg, Rube, 93, 100
Green Bin Program (Toronto), 27, 74
Green Dog Compost (OR), 14
greenhouse gases, 31

L

landfills, 90, 124, 149
    municipal solid waste (MSW), 8
    for pet waste, 74
    and sealed trash, 6, 9

M

methane gas, 32, 67, 75–76
microbes, aerobic/anaerobic, 98
microbes, mesophilic, 29, 31, 85, 133
microbes, thermophilic, 29–30, 85, 88, 91, 95, 133
Milwaukee Metropolitan Sewage District, 62
moldering, 40, 48–49, 105–9

N

National Pollutant Discharge Elimination
System (NPDES), 32
Notre-Dame-de-Grace Dog Run (Montreal), 26, 126

O

Orange County Environmental Protection
Division (OCEPD), 119

P

Pacific Dog Park (Cambridge, MA), 26
Pacific Shellfish Institute (WA), 77
Park Spark Project (Cambridge, MA), 26–27, 76
pathogens, 30–31, 38–39, 75, 119–20, 132
Pet Scoop dog waste remediation service, 141
pet septic system, 49
    See also septic systems
pet waste
    as containing nitrogen, 65
    environmental impact of, 13
    as fertilizer, 56
    handling of, 38
    recycling of, 50
pet waste compost, 40, 57
    See also composting; moldering

R

recycling, 54, 100, 124, 145, 150
refuse-derived fuel (RDF), 27
Rivanna Regional Stormwater Education Partnership (NC), 32

S

septic bins, 68, 70, 75
  See also biodigesters
septic starter, 24, 68, 70–71, 76
septic systems, 24, 29, 48, 58, 70–71, 150
septic tanks, 40, 49, 57, 60, 82, 98
sewage treatment and recovery, 39
soil amendment, 14, 40, 61, 65, 75, 97, 100, 120, 125, 131–32

T

toxoplasmosis, 37
Time magazine, 51
Tompkins County Dog Owners Group (NY), 14
Toxoplasma gondii, 23, 60
treatment plant, large waste, 43

U

upcycling, 55, 71, 78, 82, 91–92, 101, 119, 124, 142, 145, 150
US Department of Agriculture (USDA)
  Cooperative Extension, 89
  Natural Resources Conservation Service, 90, 125

V

vermicompost, 40, 117–18
vermiculture, 39–40, 48, 55, 109, 112

W

water pollution, 90
Woods End Laboratories (ME), 72
worm castings, 110, 112, 117

About the Author

Rose Seemann is the owner and operator of Enviro Wagg, a company dedicated to collecting and composting canine waste into safe, nutrient-rich garden soil. She established the company after her extensive investigations into the issue of pet waste disposal in North America uncovered an astounding labyrinth of denial, stonewalling and deception. Rose's goal is to educate and guide pet owners in the safe and responsible composting and upcycling of their dogs' and cats' waste—in doing so she hopes to nudge the world toward a more sustainable future.

If you have enjoyed *The Pet Poo Pocket Guide,* you might also enjoy other

BOOKS TO BUILD A NEW SOCIETY

Our books provide positive solutions for people who want to make a difference. We specialize in:

Sustainable Living • Green Building • Peak Oil
Renewable Energy • Environment & Economy
Natural Building & Appropriate Technology
Progressive Leadership • Resistance and Community
Educational & Parenting Resources

New Society Publishers
ENVIRONMENTAL BENEFITS STATEMENT

New Society Publishers has chosen to produce this book on recycled paper made with **100% post consumer waste,** processed chlorine free, and old growth free.

For every 5,000 books printed, New Society saves the following resources:[1]

12	Trees
1,095	Pounds of Solid Waste
1,204	Gallons of Water
1,571	Kilowatt Hours of Electricity
1,990	Pounds of Greenhouse Gases
9	Pounds of HAPs, VOCs, and AOX Combined
3	Cubic Yards of Landfill Space

[1]Environmental benefits are calculated based on research done by the Environmental Defense Fund and other members of the Paper Task Force who study the environmental impacts of the paper industry.

For a full list of NSP's titles, call 1-800-567-6772 *or visit our website* at:

www.newsociety.com

new society
PUBLISHERS